英文

日本 ...辞典

JAPAI

ILLUSTRATED
JAPANESE CHARACTERS
©1997 by JTB Publishing, Inc.
All rights reserved.

1st edition.......... Jul., 1989
15th edition.......... Feb., 2009

Printed in Japan

About this Book

1) Layout
   This book consists of the following four sections:
(1)Japanese Characters; (2) Kanji and Jukugo;
(3) Everyday Kanji; (4) Kanji Culture.

2) Japanese Words
   All the Japanese words in this book have been
romanized in accordance with the revised Hepburn
system. Except for the names of places and people, all
Japanese words are printed in italics except where
they appear in headings or bold type. Long vowels are
indicated by a line above, as in *'shintō;* and, since e's
are pronounced "ay" in Japanese, e's at the ends of
words are marked with an acute accent, as in *'saké'*
(pronounced "sahkay".)

Dear Readers

The Japanese language is known to be a very difficult language. In particular, the complex characters that are used to write Japanese are often thought by those unfamiliar with the language to be an almost insurmountable barrier to literacy. This book is an attempt to dispel that myth. It presents the kanji, Chinese characters that were adapted for use in Japan, as well as the two indigenous writing systems; hiragana and katakana, in a form that is both easy and fun to read.

This book was not designed as a comprehensive course in written Japanese. There are many books available for that purpose. The aim of this book is to help someone who has either never studied Japanese to gain a perspective on the origin, development and use of written characters in Japan, or to give the student of Japanese a way to broaden his knowledge of kanji through illustrated explanations of the meaning of fundamental kanji and common examples of their use.

The introductory pages on the history of kanji and the pages on Japanese culture and customs will be useful for anyone who is interested in Japan, whether or not he or she studies the language itself.

CONTENTS

EVERYDAY KANJI 基本の漢字

KANJI CULTURE 漢字の文化

Key

In general, *"on"* readings are given before *"kun"* readings. The letters printed in italics after each character indicate its pronunciation.

A dash "–" indicates that the following part is written in *hiragana*.

Meaning indicates the kanji's meaning.

For compound kanji, the dash represents the pronunciations of the individual kanji. The compound is however read as one word and the dash has no effect on pronunciation. Certain compounds are written without a dash. This indicates that the combination of these characters produces a reading which is unique to that combination.

An asterisk *"*"* indicates an alternate reading or meaning for one compound.

← →   means that the words on both sides are antonyms.

JAPANESE CHARACTERS
日本の文字

THE ORIGIN OF JAPANESE CHARACTERS
日本の文字のなりたち

Kanji (Chinese Characters) were developed in China in the 14th century B.C. These characters spread to the neighboring Korean Peninsula (modern-day Korea). Around the beginning of the 3rd century a man named Wani came to Japan from the ancient nation of Kudara, which was located across the Japan Sea on the eastern part of the Korean Peninsula. With him Wani brought volumes of The Analects of Confucius and *Senjimon*, a Chinese textbook for studying kanji. This was the first time that kanji were introduced to Japan. However it was not until the 4th and 5th centuries, when there was a great exchange of trade and voyagers between Japan and the Korean Peninsula, that kanji were really introduced to Japan.

The Japanese language originally developed without a form of written expression. All communication took place orally. When people wanted to tell others of an important event they hired a professional narrator known as a *kataribé*. *Kataribé* traveled around and conveyed messages and important announcements to others.

The descendants of those who immigrated to Japan worked as official recorders. They transcribed the ancient Japanese language, *Yamatokotoba*, into kanji. This provided the Japanese with their first form of written expression and allowed them to record important events and knowledge.

The use of kanji became more widespread as Chinese culture and literature spread to neighboring countries. The Korean Peninsula borders on China and many kanji and Chinese words became part of the indigenous language. In the 15th century the Korean people devised a system of characters with which to write their language. These are called Hangul letters. Today in The Republic of Korea (South Korea), Hangul characters are used in conjunction with kanji. However, kanji are not used in the Democratic People's Republic of Korea (North Korea).

Although it was in China that kanji developed over 3000 years ago, the kanji now used in China have undergone many revisions. Kanji were again abbreviated after the communist revolution in order to make them easier to read and write.

The ancient nation of Annan (modern-day Vietnam) was also greatly influenced by China. During the 3rd century, Chinese literature and kanji began to spread there as well. During the 15th century a new set of characters called Chunom were created to be used with kanji in order to adapt it to the local language. At present, the A,B,C alphabet is used in Vietnam and both kanji and Chunom have essentially disappeared.

11

Kanji

Unlike the A,B,C alphabet, which consists of phonograms (a character or symbol used to represent a word, syllable or phoneme), kanji are ideograms (a picture or symbol used to represent a thing or an idea but not a particular word or phrase for it). Each kanji was designed to express a single idea in the Chinese language. In order to express the Japanese language with these ideograms it was necessary to adapt and supplement them.

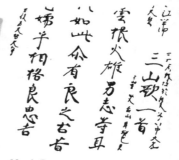

Man'yōgana

The Japanese chose kanji that were phonetically equivalent to the sounds of their *Yamatokoto-ba*. They called these characters *man'yōgana* and used them to write their language phonetically, without regard to the original character's meanings.

Hiragana and Katakana

In order to facilitate the writing process, *man'yōgana* were simplified to form *hiragana*. These new symbols were phonograms with no inherent meaning. Each one represented one of the sounds in *Yamatokotoba*. In addition to *hiragana*, another set of phonograms was created by using one portion of the *man'yōgana*. These were called *katakana*. *Hira* 平 suggests ease. Thus *hiragana* are characters that are easy to write. *Kata* 片 means incomplete. Thus, *katakana* are imcomplete *man'yōgana*. Both *hiragana* and *katakana* underwent many revisions before they were standardized as the form that appears today in modern Japanese.

Modern Japanese is written with a combination of kanji, *hiragana* and *katakana*. Kanji are used to express the basic meaning of words, whether they be nouns, verbs, adjectives or adverbs. *Hiragana* are written after kanji to modify that basic meaning and make it comform to Japanese grammatical rules.

Katakana are mainly used to write words that were originally foreign but have been incorporated into the Japanese language. Such words are called *gairaigo* 外来語, which literally means words from abroad.

Japanese sentences end with a mark that is very much like a period. It is called a *kuten* 句点 and looks like this "。". Unlike Western languages, there are no spaces between Japanese words or sentences. Question marks "?" and exclamation marks "!" are sometimes used at the end of sentences, but they are not standard.

Like Western languages, Japanese uses a punctuation mark to divide a sentence at key points in order to make it easier to read. This mark looks like this " 、" and is called a *tōten* 読点. There are no strict grammatical rules governing the use of the *tōten*.

The names of people, places and shops are usually written with kanji alone. Signs and symbols that appear in the street are also usually written not in sentence form, but with kanji alone.

KANJI
漢字

When kanji were first developed in China they were each designed to express a specific meaning or word in the Chinese language. They serve the same function in Japanese. Although Japanese can be written phonetically with both *hiragana* and *katakana*, it is the kanji, and words formed by combinations thereof, that bring meaning to what is written.

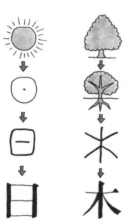

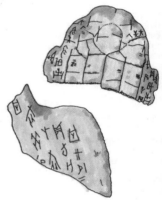

Shell and Bone Pictographs
In ancient times Chinese government officials consulted soothsayers about important matters. In the 14th century B.C. they devised a system of characters to record their advice by carving primitive pictographs on tortoise shells and animal bones. These shell and bone pictographs are the oldest kanji and the forerunner of the complex system that later developed.

The Development of Kanji
As with Egyptian hieroglyphics and other ancient writing systems, kanji began with drawings of natural objects. Such characters are called pictographs. The first kanji represented objects that were often seen in daily life. Some examples are sun 日 and tree 木.

Shell and bone pictographs

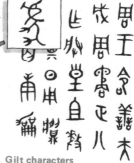

Gilt characters

These pictographs were used from the 12th century B.C. to the 3rd century A.D. They were carved on bronze ware and other tools made from metal. They were much more stable in shape than the shell and bone pictographs.

Seal characters

In the year 221 B.C. China was united under the Ch'in Emperor. At this time kanji were standardized into a universal form.

Square characters

These were abbreviated versions of the seal characters.

Print characters

These characters were more systematic than any of the others.

THE COMPOSITION OF KANJI
漢字の組み立て

In addition to pictographic kanji that are drawn based on the shape of natural objects, there are kanji that are made by combining fundamental kanji and parts thereof into new combinations with new meanings. Approximately 1900 years ago a Chinese scholar named Shushang classified kanji into the following six categories.

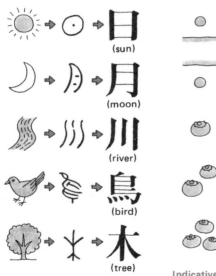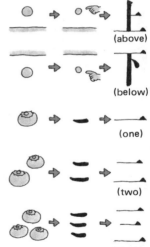

Pictographs
Few in number, these characters were made by tracing the image of natural objects.

Indicative Characters
These characters were designed based on relationships between objects. They involve abstract meanings which are linked to such relationships.

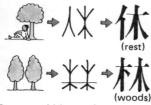

(sun) + (blue) = (clear up)

(water) + (blue) = (clean)

Compound Ideographs

By combining two or more basic kanji into a single form with a single sound and meaning, new kanji with complex and abstract meanings were created. Many consist of a section that conveys meaning and an ornamental part. Kanji that are related to people 人 use an abbreviated form of this character 亻 in their composition.

Compound Ideo-phonograms

New kanji were also created by using an abbreviated section of one kanji to express meaning and an abbreviated section of another kanji for phonetic value. Approximately 80% of all kanji were created in this way.

(gold)

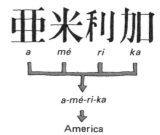

a   mé   ri   ka

a-mé-ri-ka

America

Derivative Characters

These are characters whose meaning is derived from a more fundamental kanji. For example, the character for "money" 金 also means "gold" and more fundamentally, "metal".

Substitute Characters

In situations where there was no appropriate kanji to suit an object or a concept, a character with the same pronunciation was substituted with no regard for its meaning.

HIRAGANA AND KATAKANA
ひらがなとカタカナ

These two alphabets were created by the Japanese out of the kanji that came over from China. They are phonograms with no inherent meaning. Each one represents one syllable in the Japanese language. They each represent one and only one sound.

The Origin of Hiragana

Once kanji were introduced to Japan, the Japanese people began to read Chinese literature and other texts. They attempted to write their own language with these foreign characters (*man'yō-gana*).

Many adaptations and supplements were needed to make it possible to write Japanese with kanji. *Hiragana* were one of these. *Hiragana* are written after a kanji to modify its meaning and make it conform to grammatical rules.

従二此ノ川一
船ハ可ク行ク
雖ヘド在リト
渡リ瀬別二
守ル人有リ

onnadé

During the *Heian* period (794—1185), Chinese classical literature was widely read among court nobles and aristocrats. It was during this period that the first elements of Japanese literature were written by aristocratic women. These included *tanka* and other forms of poetry as well as prose. These women did not like the rigid forms of the *man'yō-gana*. They developed simplified versions of these characters that could be written in a free-flowing style. These first *hiragana* were called *onnadé*, which literally means "women's hands". *Tanka* and other forms of literature were for the most part written by women. Thus it became customary to write them entirely in *hiragana*.

The Origin of Katakana

Katakana were formed by using one part of those kanji that were used as *man'yōgana*.

Since they are pictograms, most kanji have a complex composition. When the system of using kanji as *man'yōgana* to write Japanese was first devised in the 9th century, the original forms of the kanji were used. These were too complicated for use as a phonetic writing system. As time passed the characters were revised. They were standardized in the 10th century and called *katakana*.

katakana		kanji		hiragana
ウ ←	宇 ←	宇 →	ゔ →	う
u		u		u
カ ←	加 ←	加 →	か →	か
ka		ka		ka
ナ ←	奈 ←	奈 →	尓 →	な
na		na		na
ヒ ←	比 ←	比 →	ひ →	ひ
hi		hi		hi
レ ←	礼 ←	礼 →	れ →	れ
ré		rei		ré

Unlike *hiragana* which are used in conjunction with kanji, *katakana* are used independently. Their main use is for writing words that have entered the Japanese language from foreign languages. They are also frequently used in advertising and sometimes to replace very complicated kanji.

RULES ON HIRAGANA AND KATAKANA
かなの規則

The original Japanese language consisted of combinations of pure syllables like in the words for light 光 "hi-ka-ri" and bird 鳥 "to-ri". When the Japanese began reading Chinese literature they tried to imitate the original pronunciations. This is how inflected sounds, like "n", and compound sounds like "kya" and "gyu" entered the language.

Inflected Sound

This sound was brought into the language during the *Heian* period in order to make an inflected nasal sound. This sound is represented by ん in *hiragana* and ン in *katakana*.

新聞 しんぶん   shi-n-bu-n (newspaper)

ピンク   pi-n-ku (pink)

Palatalized Syllables

These are compound syllables that are pronounced using the palate. They are expressed by writing certain characters smaller and slightly lower than the character that represents the sound that they combine with. The *hiragana* characters are や , ゆ and よ and the *katakana* characters are ヤ , ユ and ヨ .

今日 きょう   kyō (today)

as opposed to きよう   kiyō 器用 (dexterous)

ジョージア   jō-jia (Georgia)

Geminative (Double) Consonants

Double consonants are expressed by writing a small character before a consonant. The *hiragana* character is つ and the *katakana* character is ッ .

切符 きっぷ
kippu (ticket)

コップ   koppu (cup, glass)

Voiced Consonants and Bilabial (produced with both lips) Syllables

To imitate Chinese pronunciations a device was created to alter the pronunciation of certain sounds. *ka, ki, ku, ke, ko* become *ga, gi, gu, ge, go* and *sa, shi, su, se, so* become *za, ji, zu, ze, zo.* These are called voiced consonants. Bilabial syllables are *ha, hi, hu, he, ho* which become *ba, bi, bu, be, bo* and *pa, pi, pu, pe, po.*

鈴 すず   su-zu (bell)

ダイヤモンド   daiyamondo (diamond)

パイナップル   painappuru (pineapple)

The Hiragana and Katakana

あ a	い i	う u	え e	お o	ア a	イ i	ウ u	エ e	オ o
か ka	き ki	く ku	け ke	こ ko	カ ka	キ ki	ク ku	ケ ke	コ ko
さ sa	し shi	す su	せ se	そ so	サ sa	シ shi	ス su	セ se	ソ so
た ta	ち chi	つ tsu	て te	と to	タ ta	チ chi	ツ tsu	テ te	ト to
な na	に ni	ぬ nu	ね ne	の no	ナ na	ニ ni	ヌ nu	ネ ne	ノ no
は ha	ひ hi	ふ fu	へ he	ほ ho	ハ ha	ヒ hi	フ fu	ヘ he	ホ ho
ま ma	み mi	む mu	め me	も mo	マ ma	ミ mi	ム mu	メ me	モ mo
や ya		ゆ yu		よ yo	ヤ ya		ユ yu		ヨ yo
ら ra	り ri	る ru	れ re	ろ ro	ラ ra	リ ri	ル ru	レ re	ロ ro
わ wa				を o	ワ wa				ヲ o
ん n					ン n				

TYPE STYLES
書体

The kanji used today in Japan have standardized forms. They are all print characters, but depending on how they are used their shape is often changed.

山川草木花鳥風月

kaisho (print)

山川草木花鳥風月

gyōsho (semi-cursive)

山川草木花鳥風月

sōsho (cursive)

Calligraphy
After print characters were established as the standard form in China, two other character styles were developed to make it easier to write quickly in a continuous style and to make the kanji more visually attractive. One style consisted of *gyōsho* (semi-cursive) characters and the other of *sōsho* (entirely cursive) ones.

Official Seals

Hanko are small seals with the characters for a person's or company's name engraved on them in a special design. These seals are used for official documents in the same way that Westerners sign their names on contracts and other important papers. Most people have a *hanko* made especially for them, but mass-produced *hanko* are available for the more common names. A special writing style is used in order to fit the kanji in a name on to the small space of a *hanko*. These characters are used only for seals and are called *tenkoku*.

美しい印刷書体 美しい印刷書体 美しい印刷書体 美しい印刷書体 美しい印刷書体 美しい印刷書体

Printed Characters
There are many designs used for printed matter.

NUMBERS AND UNITS
数と単位

As in Western languages, Japanese uses a decimal system based on units of ten. However, where the numerical progression in Western languages takes place every third digit, in Japan it occurs after the fourth digit. In the West the numerical progression is as follows: one, ten, one hundred, one thousand, ten thousand, one hundred thousand, one million, ten million etc. In Japan it is: one, ten, one hundred, one thousand, one *man* 万, ten *man*, one hundred *man*, one thousand *man*, one *oku* 億, ten *oku* etc.

Kanji for numbers

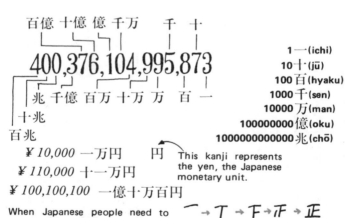

1	一 (ichi)
10	十 (jū)
100	百 (hyaku)
1000	千 (sen)
10000	万 (man)
100000000	億 (oku)
1000000000000	兆 (chō)

百億 十億 億 千万　　千　十

400,376,104,995,873

兆 千億　百万 十万 万　百 一

十兆

百兆

¥ 10,000　一万円　　　円 ← This kanji represents the yen, the Japanese monetary unit.

¥ 110,000　十一万円

¥ 100,100,100　一億十万百円

When Japanese people need to count things they often keep track by repeatedly writing the character for "correct" 正. This character is composed of five distinct strokes and is therefore convenient for counting.

一 → 丁 → 下 → 疋 → 正

I → II → III → IIII → IIII

This is very much like the Western practice of drawing four lines and then putting a line through them.

Counting objects in Japanese is quite complicated. There are different units that are used depending on what is being counted. The pronunciation of the unit depends upon the number of objects for which it is being used.

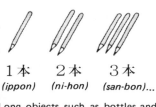

1本	2本	3本
(ippon)	*(ni-hon)*	*(san-bon)...*

Long objects such as bottles and pens are counted with the character *hon* 本.

1枚	2枚	3枚
(ichi-mai)	*(ni-mai)*	*(san-mai)...*

Thin and flat objects such as paper are counted with the character *mai* 枚.

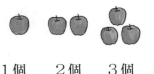

1個	2個	3個
(ikko)	*(ni-ko)*	*(san-ko)...*

Small round or square objects such as apples and dice are counted with the character *ko* 個.

1人	2人	3人
(hito-ri)	*(futa-ri)*	*(san-nin)...*

People are especially difficult to count. The character 人 is used.

1匹	2匹	3匹
(ippiki)	*(ni-hiki)*	*(san-biki)...*

Small animals such as mice or cockroaches use the character *hiki* 匹.

1軒	2軒	3軒
(ikken)	*(ni-ken)*	*(san-ken)...*

Houses use the character *ken* 軒.

ON AND KUN READINGS
音と訓

For each kanji used in the Japanese language there are two or more possible pronunciations. These are divided into *on* readings and *kun* readings.

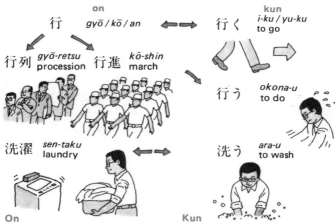

on
行　*gyō / kō / an*　⟷　行く　**kun** *i-ku / yu-ku* to go

行列　*gyō-retsu* procession　　行進　*kō-shin* march

行う　*okona-u* to do

洗濯　*sen-taku* laundry　⟷　洗う　*ara-u* to wash

On

A kanji's *on* readings are based on the original pronunciation of that character in the Chinese language. Most kanji have several *on* readings. The reason for this is that kanji were not brought over to Japan and standardized immediately. Each *on* reading represents a different period when that character was transmitted to Japan. The correct *on* reading for each kanji depends upon the kanji with which it is combined to form a word.

Kun

Kun readings represent a kanji whose original meaning was expressed with the indigenous Japanese language. It was necessary to add *hiragana* to the kanji in order to adapt them to the Japanese language. As with *on* readings, most kanji have several *kun* readings which can be differentiated by the *hiragana* which follow them and by the context in which they are used. One *kun* reading can often also be written by several different kanji.

KANJI
AND
JUKUGO
漢字と熟語

KANJI COMPOUNDS
熟語の構造

Kanji are generally combined in groups of two or more in order to form single more complex concepts. These compounds are called *jukugo* 熟語 . Exceptions aside, *jukugo* can be classified into 5 categories depending on the relationship of the formative kanji.

Active Relationship

A does or is B

A = the earth

B = to shake

AB = earthquake *(ji-shin)*

A = year

B = long

AB = older/senior *(nen-chō)*

Modifying Relationship

A modifies B

A = good

B = person

AB = good/moral people *(zen-nin)*

A = violent

B = to move

AB = turbulence/agitation *(geki-dō)*

28

Parallel Relationship

A and B have similar meanings and reinforce each other

A = soil 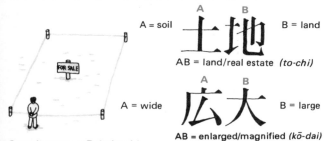 B = land

AB = land/real estate *(to-chi)*

A = wide B = large

AB = enlarged/magnified *(kō-dai)*

Complementary Relationship

B complements A

A = to seek B = person

AB = Help Wanted/job vacancy *(kyū-jin)*

A = to ride B = car

AB = to board (a vehicle) *(jō-sha)*

Confirmatory Relationship

A acknowledges or rejects B

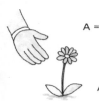

A = obligation B = sympathize

AB = poor/pitiful/sweet *(ka-ren)*

A = negation B = correct/just

AB = unjust/wrong *(fu-sei)*

Meaning
up, top portion, superior, to raise, to rise, to climb

(jō, ué, kami, a-geru, nobo-ru)

This character has a horizontal line as a base from which it rises, thereby expressing the notion of "up".

Meaning
middle, inside, center, underway, neutral

(chū, naka)

With a line drawn directly through the center of a box, this kanji represents the idea of "middle".

Meaning
bottom, under, origin, vulgar, low, to descend

(ka, gé, shita, shimo, moto, kuda-ru, sa-geru, o-riru)

The opposite of 上, this character descends from its horizontal line to express the concept of "underneath".

(jō-ryū)
上流
upstream, upper class

→ 中流
(chū-ryū)
midstream, middle class

(jō-hin)
上品
high quality, elegant

←→ 下品
(gé-hin)
low quality, crude

(shita-gokoro)
下心
ulterior motive

(gé-zai)
下剤
laxative

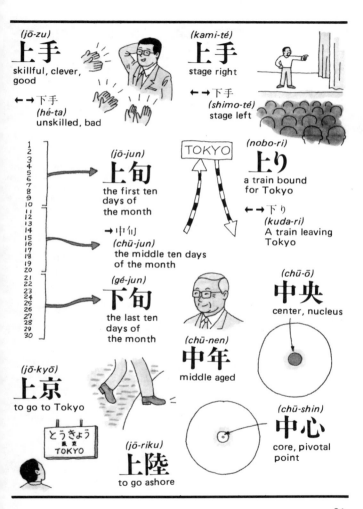

(jō-zu)
上手
skillful, clever, good

←→ 下手
(hé-ta)
unskilled, bad

(kami-té)
上手
stage right

←→ 下手
(shimo-té)
stage left

(jō-jun)
上旬
the first ten days of the month

→中旬
(chū-jun)
the middle ten days of the month

(gé-jun)
下旬
the last ten days of the month

TOKYO

(nobo-ri)
上り
a train bound for Tokyo

←→ 下り
(kuda-ri)
A train leaving Tokyo

(chū-ō)
中央
center, nucleus

(chū-nen)
中年
middle aged

(jō-kyō)
上京
to go to Tokyo

とうきょう
東京
TOKYO

(jō-riku)
上陸
to go ashore

(chū-shin)
中心
core, pivotal point

内

Meaning
inside, internal

(nai, dai, uchi)

Composed of the character for "enter" 入 located inside an enclosure 冂 , this kanji originally meant entrance.

外

Meaning
other, outside, foreign, to remove

(gai, gé, hoka, soto)

This kanji contains the notions of a cracking sound and the character for "divination" 卜 . In ancient times soothsayers examined the cracked lines that appear on burnt tortoise shells in order to predict the future. Thus arose this kanji's concept of "surface" and "exterior".

(nai-sen)

内線
telephone extension

(nai-huku-yaku)

内服薬
medicine taken internally

(nai-kaku)

内閣
ministerial cabinet

(nai-ran)

内乱
civil war

(nai-mitsu)

内密
confidential

(nai-ka)

内科
internal medicine

← → 外科
(gé-ka)
surgery

(jō-nai)

場内
in the hall

(gai-jin)
外人
foreigner

(gai-koku)
外国
foreign country

(gai-kō)
外交
diplomacy

(gai-rai-go)
外来語
foreign word

(kai-gai)
海外
abroad

(gai-sha)
外車
foreign automobile

コーヒー スープ
ジュース ウィスキー
ワイン ミルク

(jo-gai)
除外
to exclude

(gai-kan)
外観
external appearance

(gai-yō)
外用
for external use

(nai-shin)
内心
inward, one's mind

外 and 内 are related to an object's location. 表 (front) and 裏 (rear) convey the notion of things that are or are not visible.

入
Meaning
to enter

(nyū, i-ru, hai-ru)

This kanji is shaped like an entrance and contains the basic meaning of "enter".

出
Meaning
to go out of something, to appear

(shutsu, dé-ru, da-su)

The original character had feet coming out of an entrance. Conveys the idea of leaving or pushing out.

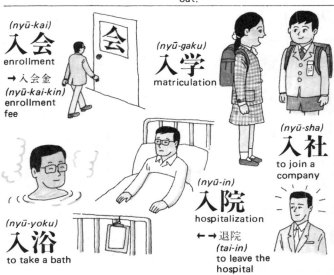

(nyū-kai)
入会
enrollment
→ 入会金
(nyū-kai-kin)
enrollment fee

(nyū-gaku)
入学
matriculation

(nyū-sha)
入社
to join a company

(nyū-in)
入院
hospitalization
← → 退院
(tai-in)
to leave the hospital

(nyū-yoku)
入浴
to take a bath

(shusshin)
出身
to come from,
to graduate
from

(shussan)
出産
to bear a child

(shuppan)
出版
to publish

hometown

BOOK

(dé-ki)
出来
workmanship,
crop

(shusseki)
出席
to attend
← → 欠席
(kesseki)
absent

(yu-shutsu)
輸出
to export
← → 輸入
(yu-nyū)
to import

(shukka)
出火
outbreak of
fire

(shussé)
出世
to succeed

EXECUTIVE

INPORT

(i-ri-é)
入り江
inlet, bay

(iri-guchi)
入口
entrance
← → 出口
(dé-guchi)
exit

入口

(nyū-shu)
入手
procurement

35

Meaning
east

(tō, higashi, azuma)

The original shape of this kanji represented a bag that is bound from top to bottom. Since the direction from which the sun rose was called *"tō"*, this character came to represent "east".

Meaning
west

(sei, sai, nishi)

This character is based on the shape of a crate used to squeeze rice when making *saké* 酒 . The parallel between the liquid dripping from the crate and the sun descending in the sky led to the character's use to express "west".

Meaning
south

(nan, minami)

Originally this kanji indicated the warmer side of a house. This led to its use as "south".

Meaning
north

(hoku, kita)

The model for this character was a person with his back turned. In China houses were built facing south, so their back was to the north.

(tō-zai-nan-boku)
東西南北
the four directions

(kan-tō)
関東
eastern district
around Tokyo

←→関西
(kan-sai)
western district
around Osaka

(tō-kyō)
東京
Tokyo (the
eastern capital)

(tō-yō)
東洋
the Orient

←→西洋
(sei-yō)
the Occident

(higashi-guchi)
東口
east exit

→西口 **(nishi-guchi)**
west exit
南口 **(minami-guchi)**
south exit
北口 **(kita-guchi)**
north exit

(tō-hon-sei-sō)
東奔西走
to be on the go

(sei-reki)
西暦
Christian Era,
A.D.

(nan-kyoku)
南極
South Pole

←→北極
(hokkyoku)
North Pole

(minami-kazé)
南風
south wind

←→北風
(kita-kazé)
north wind

(nan-goku)
南国
a southern
country

(nan-ka)
南下
to go south

(hoku-i)
北緯
North latitude

(hai-boku)
敗北
defeat

前
(zen, maé)

Meaning
front, head,
before, previous

後
*(go, kō, nochi,
ato, ushi-ro,
oku-reru)*

Meaning
rear, afterwards,
to be late, future

The original meaning of this character was to cut and arrange. It was next used to express ''proceed'' and from there it took on the meaning for front.

Originally this character meant ''to return''. This led to the meaning of ''retreat''.

(zen-pō)
前方
front

←→ 後方
(kō-hō)
back

(zen-jitsu)
前日
the day before

昨日
(saku-jitsu)
yesterday

(zen-ya)
前夜
the previous night

START

(zen-han)
前半
first half

←→ 後半
(kō-han)
second half

GOAL

(maé-uri)
前売
advance sale

0.1
8.7
9.1
9.3
9.6
9.9
0

(zen-go)
前後
approximately

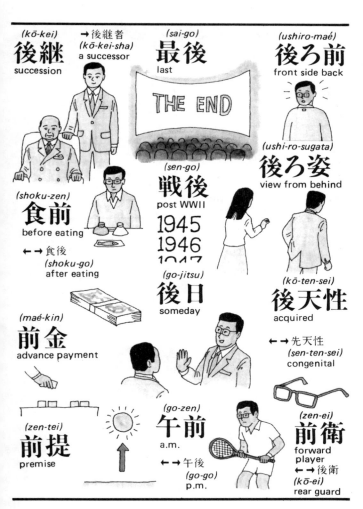

(kō-kei)
後継
succession

→ 後継者
(kō-kei-sha)
a successor

(sai-go)
最後
last

(ushiro-maé)
後ろ前
front side back

(ushi-ro-sugata)
後ろ姿
view from behind

(sen-go)
戦後
post WWII

1945
1946
1947

(shoku-zen)
食前
before eating

←→ 食後
(shoku-go)
after eating

(go-jitsu)
後日
someday

(kō-ten-sei)
後天性
acquired

←→ 先天性
(sen-ten-sei)
congenital

(maé-kin)
前金
advance payment

(zen-tei)
前提
premise

(go-zen)
午前
a.m.

←→ 午後
(go-go)
p.m.

(zen-ei)
前衛
forward
player
←→ 後衛
(kō-ei)
rear guard

39

大

Meaning
large, wide, praiseworthy

(tai, dai, ō-kii)

The shape of a person with his arms and legs fully extended indicates great size.

小

Meaning
small, little, trivial, young, unimportant

(shō, ko, o, chii-sai)

Three short lines indicate smallness.

中

See page 30.

(ō-ya)
大家
landlord

(tai-shū)
大衆
the masses

(otona)
大人
adult

← → 小人
(kodomo)
child

(dai-butsu)
大仏
large image of Buddha

(tai-kai)
大会
convention

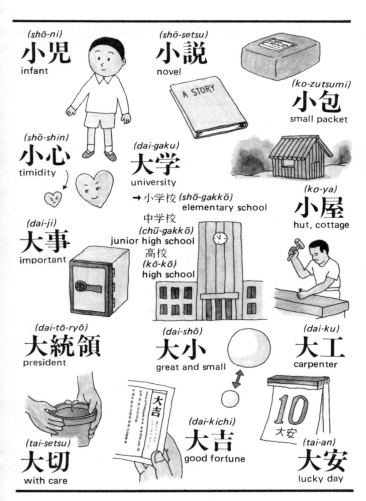

(shō-ni)
小児
infant

(shō-setsu)
小説
novel

(ko-zutsumi)
小包
small packet

(shō-shin)
小心
timidity

(dai-gaku)
大学
university

→ 小学校 *(shō-gakkō)*
elementary school

中学校
(chū-gakkō)
junior high school

高校
(kō-kō)
high school

(ko-ya)
小屋
hut, cottage

(dai-ji)
大事
important

(dai-tō-ryō)
大統領
president

(dai-shō)
大小
great and small

(dai-ku)
大工
carpenter

(tai-setsu)
大切
with care

(dai-kichi)
大吉
good fortune

(tai-an)
大安
lucky day

左
(sa, hidari)

Meaning
left, to help, inferior (in ancient times the right side was considered to be better), low status, contrary, evil

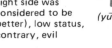

This kanji is drawn in the shape of the left hand. As the left hand was considered a helper 佐 for the right hand, the original meaning of this character was "to help".

右
(yū, u, migi)

Meaning
right, to help, nearby, to respect

The original word for the right hand was "yū". This kanji was given that meaning as well as the idea of leading and helping others.

(sa-sen)
左遷
demotion

(sa-yū)
左右
left and right, nearby, alongside, to sway

(migi-mawa-ri)
右回り
clockwise

(u-ō-sa-ō)
右往左往
to go hither and thither

天
(ten, amê, ama)

Meaning
sky, heaven, congenital, god, natural

This character originally had a head directly above a person to express the heavens. Later it came to mean the skies, fate, and developments as a result of human action.

(ten-ka)
天下
the world, ruling power

(ten-sai)
天才
prodigy

(ten-sai)
天災
natural calamity

(ten-jō)
天井
the ceiling

(ten-ki)
天気
weather

(ten-chi)
天地
heaven and the earth, a great difference

(ten-goku)
天国
heaven

(ten-shi)
天使
angel

43

KANJI THAT EXPRESS BASIC CONCEPTS

高
(kō, taka-i)

Meaning
high, noble,
excellence of spirit
and character,
to age, an object's
volume

低
(tei, hiku-i)

Meaning
low, cheap, to hang,
to descend

This kanji originally indicated "looking up at a high building".

This kanji originally meant "bottom", before it took on the meaning of "low".

(taka-dai)
高台
hill

(kō-atsu)
高圧
high pressure,
high tension

(kō-ka)
高架
elevated

(kō-on)
高音
high tone

←→低音
(tei-on)
bass

(kō-on)
高温
high
temperature

←→低温
(tei-on)
low temperature

HOT!

(kō-kyū)
高級
high rank

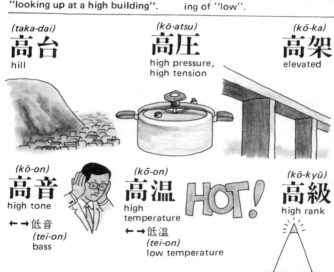

44

(tei-kū)
低空
low altitude

(sai-tei)
最低
minimum

←→最高
(sai-kō)
maximum

(tei-ka)
低下
to decline

(tei-retsu)
低劣
inferior

(tei-mei)
低迷
depression

(tei-chō)
低調
dullness

(kō-do)
高度
high altitude,
advanced

(kō-tei)
高低
modulation

(kō-soku)
高速
high speed

→高速道路
(kō-soku-dō-ro)
highway

(kō-mei)
高名
fame

(kō-ki-atsu)
高気圧
high atmospheric
pressure

←→低気圧
(tei-ki-atsu)
low atmospheric
pressure

(kō-ka)
高価
high price

(kō-kan)
高官
high officer

高
1016

高
1026

非
(hi, ara-zu)

Meaning
bad, incorrect, to blame, to criticize, to deceive, to deny, negation

否
(hi, ina)

Meaning
to deny, to disagree, wrong, to block

This character was modeled on the image of flapping wings.

By adding a mouth 口 to 不, its meaning is reinforced.

不
(fu, zu)

Meaning
when attached as a prefix this character expresses negation or prohibition

minus

無
(mu, bu, na-i)

Meaning
not, prohibition, when attached as a prefix this indicates a lack of that which follows.

ZE O RO

The sound "fu" expresses negation. This character is a phonetic derivation of a character that is drawn from the image of a flower pedal with small green leaves.

This character is a phonetic derivation of a kanji that was drawn from the image of a person dancing.

(hi-jō-shiki)
非常識

常識 means "common-sense". Add 非 and it means "absurd" and "thoughtless".

(hi-jō-guchi)
非常口

常 means "normal". This combination means "emergency exit".

46

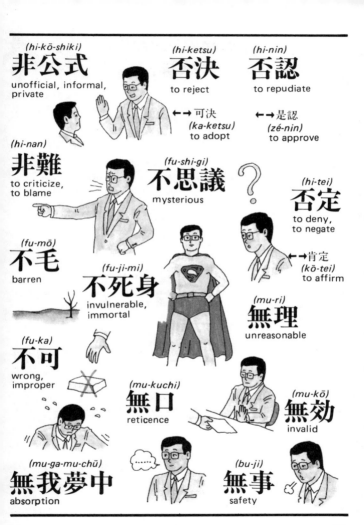

(hi-kō-shiki)
非公式
unofficial, informal, private

(hi-ketsu)
否決
to reject

(hi-nin)
否認
to repudiate

←→ 可決
(ka-ketsu)
to adopt

←→ 是認
(zé-nin)
to approve

(hi-nan)
非難
to criticize, to blame

(fu-shi-gi)
不思議
mysterious

(hi-tei)
否定
to deny, to negate

(fu-mō)
不毛
barren

(fu-ji-mi)
不死身
invulnerable, immortal

←→ 肯定
(kō-tei)
to affirm

(mu-ri)
無理
unreasonable

(fu-ka)
不可
wrong, improper

(mu-kuchi)
無口
reticence

(mu-kō)
無効
invalid

(mu-ga-mu-chū)
無我夢中
absorption

(bu-ji)
無事
safety

STROKE ORDER
書き順

When writing kanji there are certain rules governing the order of the strokes. These rules were laid out in ancient times and are the best and fastest way of writing.

The following are basic rules on stroke order.

1. Top to Bottom

Always draw the top strokes and then proceed down.

2. Left to Right

Always draw the left part of a kanji before the right part.

丶 → 亠 → 宀 → 宁 → 高 → 盲 → 高 → 高 → 高 → 高

丿 → 刂 → 川 → 川 → 川 → 川 → 順 → 順 → 順 → 順 → 順

3. Horizontal to Vertical

Always draw lines that go from left to right before lines that go from top to bottom.

4. Inside to Outside

Always draw the inside of a box before closing it.

一 → ナ → 大

丨 → 冂 → 冂 → 冃 → 用 → 国 → 国 → 国

When drawing kanji it is important to keep in mind that certain strokes should end abruptly with a thick line, some should end gradually coming to a thin point and others should end with a hook.

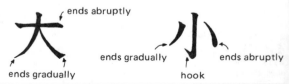

ends abruptly

ends gradually

ends gradually   ends abruptly

hook

48

EVERYDAY KANJI

基本の漢字

san, sen, yama

This pictographic kanji is modeled on towering mountain peaks.

Meaning mountain, high altitude, objects that are piled high, peaks of adventurous work

This character is used in compound kanji that are related to mountains and other geographic phenomena related to differences in elevation.

富士山
(fu-ji-san)
Mt. Fuji

''*san*'' is attached to mountain names. (Not related to the ''*san*'' (Mr./Mrs.) that follows people's names.)

山脈
(san-myaku)
mountain range

Since *myaku* 脈 means a series of objects, we combine it with 山 to form this compound.

登山
(to-zan)
mountain climbing

山陽新幹線
(san-yō-shin-kan-sen)
Shinkansen (bullet train) from Osaka to Fukuoka

San'yō 山陽 means a mountain's southern side. The southern portion of the area, west of Osaka on Japan's main island, or *Honshū* is called the San'yō Region.

50

岳
(gaku, také)
peak, mountain

This kanji developed from the image of mountains towering over other mountains. Essentially the same as 山, this kanji implies a high, majestic mountain.

山岳
(san-gaku)
mountains

岩
(gan, iwa)
rock

This kanji combines the character for mountain with that for stone 石.

岩石
(gan-seki)
rock, crag

夫婦岩
(meoto-iwa)
A place in Japan of religious significance where two stones are connected with a straw bridge to signify marital piety.

島
(tō, shima)
island

The lower portion of the character for bird 鳥 was replaced with a mountain to form this kanji. Just as birds float across the sky, islands float above the sea.

島流し
(shima-naga-shi)
banishment to a deserted island for criminals

日本列島
(ni-hon-rettō)
the Japanese Archipelago

嵐
(ran, arashi)

This character combines a mountain with the kanji for wind 風 to express the idea of a storm.

砂嵐
(suna-arashi)
sandstorm

嵐山
(arashi-yama)
a well-known mountain near Kyoto

峠
(tōgé)
mountain pass

By combining ascent 上 and descent 下 with a mountain we have the idea for the space between mountains. From here came this character's meaning of "limit" and "summit".

峠の茶屋 *(tōgé-no-cha-ya)*
mountain tea hut

岸
(gan, kishi)
shore, coast, bank

Beginning with the meaning of a high mountain, this kanji took on the idea of a high shore alongside a coast. It now simply indicates a shoreline.

岸壁
(gan-peki)
quay, wharf, breakwater

海岸
(kai-gan)
seacoast

湾岸道路
(wan-gan-dō-ro)
a road that follows the coast

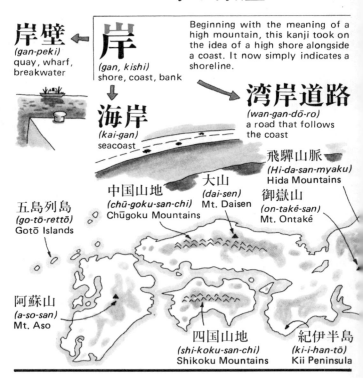

飛驒山脈
(Hi-da-san-myaku)
Hida Mountains

大山
(dai-sen)
Mt. Daisen

御嶽山
(on-také-san)
Mt. Ontaké

中国山地
(chū-goku-san-chi)
Chūgoku Mountains

五島列島
(go-tō-rettō)
Gotō Islands

阿蘇山
(a-so-san)
Mt. Aso

四国山地
(shi-koku-san-chi)
Shikoku Mountains

紀伊半島
(ki-i-han-tō)
Kii Peninsula

Important Japanese Mountains and Islands

大雪山
(dai-setsu-zan)
Mt. Daisetsu

知床半島
(Shiré-toko-han-tō)
Shiretoko Peninsula

積丹半島
(shako-tan-han-tō)
Shakotan Peninsula

岩手山
(iwa-té-san)
Mt. Iwaté

鳥海山
(chō-kai-san)
Mt. Chōkai

日高山脈
(hi-daka-san-myaku)
Hidaka Mountains

佐渡島
(sa-do-ga-shima)
Sado Island

襟裳岬
(eri-mo-misaki)
Erimo Point

登半島
(o-to-han-tō)
oto Peninsula

奥羽山脈
(ō-u-san-myaku)
Ōu Mountains

磐梯山
(ban-dai-san)
Mt. Bandai

谷川岳
(tani-gawa-daké)
Mt. Tanigawa

妙高山
(myō-kō-san)
Mt. Myōkō

白根山
(shira-né-san)
Mt. Shirané

浅間山
(asa-ma-yama)
Mt. Asama

乗鞍岳
(nori-kura-daké)
Mt. Norikura

三原山
(mi-hara-yama)
Mt. Mihara

富士山
(fu-ji-san)
Mt. Fuji

sui, mizu

水

This kanji combines the shape of a current 〔 with water 氵. It originally expressed flowing water.

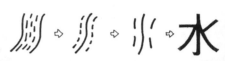

Meaning water, horizontal, flat

When used in compounds this kanji is abbreviated to this form 氵 and is called the *"sanzui"* element. Compounds that use it are related to water, currents, rivers, oceans, waves and other similar concepts.

海水
(kai-sui)
seawater

The same compositional concept allows for similar compounds such as 塩水 *(shio-mizu)* which means "saltwater" and 香水 *(kō-sui)* which means perfume.

水泳
(sui-ei)
swimming

水色
(mizu-iro)
light blue

水色

水平
(sui-hei)
horizontal

→ 水平線
(sui-hei-sen)
the horizon

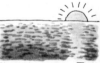

The character 平 is used to describe anything that, like the surface of a body of water, is truly horizontal.

氷
(hyō, kōri)
ice

The original kanji was based on the image of frozen ice crystals. Means "ice", "freezing" and "clear and transparent objects".

氷山
(hyō-zan)
iceberg

氷いちご
(kōri-i-chi-go)
shaved ice with strawberry syrup

求
(kyū, moto-meru)
to seek

This kanji was originally modeled on a hanging fur. Because furs were highly valued objects it took on the meaning of "to seek" and "to desire".

求人広告
(kyū-jin-kō-koku)
a want ad

汁
(jū, shiru)
soup, juice

Originally this kanji had the meaning of "to mix". It is now used for gravy, soup and sauces.

味噌汁
(mi-so-shiru)
fermented bean paste soup

決勝戦
(kesshō-sen)
championship match

果汁
(ka-jū)
fruit juice

決
(ketsu, kimé-ru)

Originally this character expressed the image of water bursting forth from behind a dike. It also conveys the ideas of "to take care of" and "to decide".

決定
(kettei)
decision

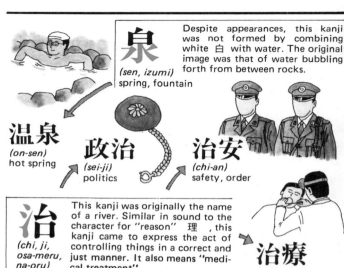

泉
(sen, izumi)
spring, fountain

Despite appearances, this kanji was not formed by combining white 白 with water. The original image was that of water bubbling forth from between rocks.

温泉
(on-sen)
hot spring

政治
(sei-ji)
politics

治安
(chi-an)
safety, order

治
(chi, ji, osa-meru, na-oru)
to govern, to regulate, to cure

This kanji was originally the name of a river. Similar in sound to the character for "reason" 理 , this kanji came to express the act of controlling things in a correct and just manner. It also means "medical treatment".

治療
(chi-ryō)
medical treatment

石油
(seki-yu)
petroleum

サラダ油
(sa-ra-da-yu)
salad oil

油断
(yu-dan)
negligence
In ancient times, the keeper of oil had a great responsibility. If he was careless with his job he was killed.

油
(yu, abura)
oil

This character originally expressed a current gushing forth. It came to mean "oil" in modern times.

酒
(shu, saké)
saké, alcohol

Formed from a *sanzui* 氵 and the character for a jar 壹, this kanji is used with alcoholic beverages.

日本酒
(ni-hon-shu)
Japanese saké

お神酒
(o-mi-ki)
holy saké

居酒屋
(i-zaka-ya)
bar

洗濯
(sen-taku)
laundry

洗
(sen, ara-u)
to wash

Originally this kanji meant "to wash the feet". This meaning spread to a general meaning of "washing" and "cleanliness". Used to indicate the process of soaking raw fish in Japanese cooking.

洗面所
(sen-men-jo)
toilet

横浜港
(yoko-hama-kō)
Yokohama Port

港
(kō, minato)
port, harbor

This kanji was based on the ancient word for waterway.

湖畔
(ko-han)
lake shore

湖
(ko, mizuumi)
lake

By combining a *sanzui* with a character meaning "large", we have the idea for a large body of water; a lake.

洋
(yō)
ocean, Occidental

This kanji was originally designed to mean "large and wide". From here it took on the nuances of "ocean" "Occident" and "great expanse".

太平洋
(tai-hei-yō)
the Pacific Ocean

洋式
(yō-shiki)
Western style

洋服
(yō-fuku)
Western style clothes

消火器
(shō-ka-ki)
fire extinguisher

消
(shō, ki-eru, ké-su)
to disappear, to erase

A *sanzui* was combined with a character meaning "to reduce" to form the meaning of a flow of water slowing down and stopping. It was later adapted to a wider range of things.

消防署
(shō-bō-sho)
fire department

消火栓
(shō-ka-sen)
fire hydrant

消費者
(shō-hi-sha)
consumer

湯
(tō, yu)
hot water

A *sanzui* was combined with a character for warm to create this kanji. This also means "overflowing".

銭湯
(sen-tō)
public bath

58

浴
(yoku, a-biru)
to shower

This character basically expresses the idea of pouring water over the body. In addition, it can mean directly receiving things and putting something directly on the head.

日光浴
(nikkō-yoku)
to sunbathe

入浴
(nyū-yoku)
to bathe

浴室
(yoku-shitsu)
bathroom

流
(ryū, ru, naga-reru)
to flow

The combination of a *sanzui* with the image of a child's birth form this kanji. In addition to the idea of a current, this character expresses "without foundation", "broad" and "to transmit".

流行
(ryū-kō)
fashion, vogue

流氷
(ryū-hyō)
an ice flow

一流
(ichi-ryū)
top level

流し
(naga-shi)
a sink, a wanderer

人

jin, nin, hito

This pictograph was modeled on the image of a person standing up.

Meaning person, people, others, respectable people, personality, the unit used for counting people.

When abbreviated for use with compounds it looks like this ⺅ and is called the *"nimben"* element.

人間
(nin-gen)
people,
human beings

→ 人間性
(nin-gen-sei)
humanity

人気
(nin-ki)
popularity
*(hito-ké)
populated

人生
(jin-sei)
life

LIFE!

この人
(ko-no-hito)
this person

→ その人
(so-no-hito)
that person

今
(kon, kin, ima)
now

This kanji shows an object underneath a roof. It was given the meaning of "now" from the ancient word for time.

今日
(kyō)
today

→ **今年**
(ko-toshi)
this year

今月
(kon-getsu)
this month

今夜
(kon-ya)
tonight

今朝
(ké-sa)
this morning

仏教
(bukkyō)
Buddhism

仏語
(futsu-go)
The French language

仏
(butsu, futsu, hotoké)
Buddhism

When Buddhism was introduced to China, the phonographic compound of 佛陀 was created to express the idea of "Buddha". 佛 is the original form for 仏. This character is also used to represent France. (See page 65.)

仕
(shi, tsuka-eru)
civil service, work

Originally used for public officials, this kanji is now used for all kinds of work, but especially for respected and noble positions.

仕事
(shi-goto)
work

仕入れ
(shi-i-ré)
to purchase the stock

個
(ko, ka)

Used as a counter for individual units.

個人
(ko-jin)
individual

→ **1個**
(ikko)
one

→ **2個、**
(ni-ko)
two

3個……
(san-ko)
three

他
(ta, hoka)
other

Originally this character was the same as 佗, which means "peace without snakes" (which represent evil). It is now used to express "other", "different" and "foreign".

→ **その他**
(so-no-ta)
in addition to

他人 ←
(ta-nin)
other people

代表
(dai-hyō)
representative

時代 ←
(ji-dai)
era

代
(dai, yo, kawa-ru)
represent

This kanji originally meant "to switch places". It expanded to include the notions of "represent", "generation" and "exchange".

交代
(kō-tai)
to trade places

休
(kyū, yasu-mu)
to rest

The combination of a person and a tree 木 suggests someone resting in the shade. Other meanings include "to stop", "to sleep" and "to quit".

→ **休日**
(kyū-jitsu)
holiday

体
(tai, tei, karada)
the body

The original character 體 stood for the entire body. 体 now means "body", "mold", "setting" and "core".

体重
(tai-jū)
body weight

仲間
(naka-ma)
associate

仲
(chū, naka)
relationship

Originally this kanji was used for "middle child". It now is used to express relationships between people and for intermediary things.

仲人
(nakō-do)
a matchmaker

仲介
(chū-kai)
intermediation

住
(jū, su-mu)
to reside

Originally derived from the word for "to stop" and "to reside", this kanji now indicates living in a fixed residence.

住所
(jū-sho)
address

住宅
(jū-taku)
residence

価値
(ka-chi)
value

スーツ
¥300,000

価格
(ka-kaku)
price

スーツ
¥25,000

特価
(tokka)
special price

¥10,000
3,000

価
(ka, atai)
value, price

The combination of a *ninben* with a segment indicating "trade" gives this kanji the meaning of "monetary value" and "price".

来
(rai, ku-ru)
to come

This pictographic character was modeled from the image of leaves of wheat hanging in the wind. Perhaps the notion that wheat was helped by god led to the use of this character for "to come".

来日
(rai-nichi)
to come to Japan

来年
(rai-nen)
next year

next

→ **来月** **来週**
(rai-getsu) *(rai-shū)*
next month next week

係長
(kakari-chō)
chief clerk

係
(kei, kaka-ru)
duty, relation

The combination of a *ninben* and a section that indicates "joining", gives this kanji the meaning of relations between people and things. When used in a work context it indicates someone in charge of something.

便利
(ben-ri)
convenient

便
(ben, bin, tayori)
convenience, mail

Originally derived from the ancient word for controlling things, this kanji's meanings include "assistant", "good circumstances", "convenient" and "mail".

郵便局
(yū-bin-kyoku)
post office

便所
(ben-jo)
toilet

俳優
(hai-yū)
actor

優先
(yū-sen)
priority

優
(yū, yasa-shii)
superior, gentle

The combination of a *ninben* and an entertainer represented ancient performers. From there this kanji took on the meaning of "elegant", "abundant", "excellent" and "gentle".

Located to the east of China, Japan was called "the land of the rising sun" 日本 . 日 means "sun" and 本 means "root or source". 日 is often used in compounds to mean "Japan".

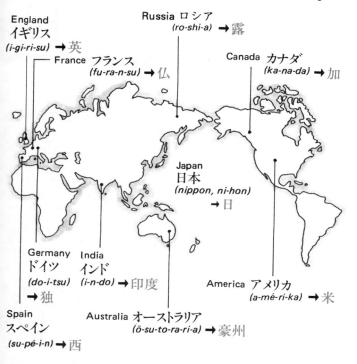

England
イギリス
(i-gi-ri-su) ➡ 英

Russia ロシア
(ro-shi-a) ➡ 露

France フランス
(fu-ra-n-su) ➡ 仏

Canada カナダ
(ka-na-da) ➡ 加

Japan
日本
(nippon, ni-hon)
➡ 日

Germany
ドイツ
(do-i-tsu)
➡ 独

India
インド
(i-n-do) ➡ 印度

America アメリカ
(a-mé-ri-ka) ➡ 米

Spain
スペイン
(su-pé-i-n) ➡ 西

Australia オーストラリア
(ō-su-to-ra-ri-a) ➡ 豪州

As they are essentially *gairaigo* 外来語 (see p. 13), names of foreign countries are usually written in *katakana*, but there are kanji for some countries.

jitsu, nichi, hi

日

This pictographic character was modeled on the image of the shining sun.

Meaning sun, sunshine, afternoon, one day, the counter for days

日記
(nikki)
diary

記 means "to record". A 日記 is a recording of each day's events.

毎日
(mai-nichi)
every day

毎 means "each". This compound therefore means "every day". In the same way we have 毎週 *(mai-shū)* every week, 毎月 *(mai-tsuki)* every month and 毎年 *(mai-toshi)* every year.

元日
(gan-jitsu)
New Year's Day

元 is modeled after a person's head. It means "beginning", "source" and "origin". This compound means the first day of the year.
元年 *(gan-nen)* means the first year of a historical era.

日光
(nikkō)
sunshine

光 means beam. Nikkō 日光 is also the name of a well-known area near Tokyo.

早
(sō, haya-i)
early

This combination of the sun and an element meaning "to open" originally meant "sunrise". It is now used to express "early" or "fast". It has a homophone (words pronounced alike but different in meaning):

早朝
(sō-chō)
early morning

速い *(haya-i)*
This character is used to express "quick" and "fast". Both 早 and 速 are opposites of 遅い *(oso-i)*, which means both "late" and "slow".

時計
(to-kei)
watch

時間
(ji-kan)
time

時
(ji, toki)
time, hour

Derived from the ancient word for "to move", this kanji takes its meaning from the sun's motion, which is used to count the passing of time.

当時
(tō-ji)
at that time

証明
(shō-mei)
to certify

明
(mei, myō, aki-raka, a-keru, aka-rui)
bright, clear, tomorrow, dawn

The combination of the sun and the moon 月 indicates brightness and the clarity that vision provides.

発明
(hatsu-mei)
invention

照明
(shō-mei)
to illuminate

明日
(ashita, asu, myō-nichi)
tomorrow

→ 明朝 *(myō-chō)*
tomorrow morning

The opposite of 明 is 暗 *(an, kura-i)* darkness.

暗示	暗記	暗黙
(an-ji)	*(an-ki)*	*(an-moku)*
hint	memorization	tacit

昨
(saku)
yester-

The original meaning of this kanji was "to pile up". Since one day is piled on to the next, this kanji took on the meaning of "yesterday" and "the past".

昨日
*(kinō
saku-jitsu)
yesterday

昨年 = **去年**
(saku-nen) *(kyo-nen)*
last year

YESTERDAY

新春
(shin-shun)
the beginning
of the year

春
(shun, haru)
spring

This kanji is modeled on the image of the sun and mulberry flowers 桑 growing longer. As we enter the spring both the sun and flowers grow longer.

YOUTH

青春
(sei-shun)
youth

小春日和
(ko-haru-bi-yori)
Indian summer

星座
(sei-za)
constellation

星占い
(hoshi-urana-i)
astrology

星
*(sei, shō,
hoshi)*
star

The 日 in this character is the abbreviated version of the character for "crystal" 晶. Just as crystal shines, this kanji represents shining heavenly bodies.

昼食
(chū-shoku)
lunch

昼
(chū, hiru)
afternoon

Originally this character meant "brightness". Later on it was adapted to express the brightest part of the day.

昼休み
(hiru-yasu-mi)
lunch break

晴天
(sei-ten)
fair weather

晴れ着
(ha-ré-gi)
one's best clothes

晴
(sei, ha-reru)
to clear up

The combination of a sun and an element meaning "to open" indicates the clearing up of clouds in the sky to reveal the sun. It is also used to express something done openly before people; "public".

今晩
(kon-ban)
tonight

晩婚
(ban-kon)
late marriage

← → 早婚 *(sō-kon)*
early marriage

晩
(ban)
night

Based on the ancient word for "sunset", this character is used to mean both "night" and "late".

映画
(ei-ga)
movie

映
(ei, utsu-ru, ha-eru)
to reflect

This character was based on an image of the sun's reflection and was adapted to mean "reflect", "illuminate" and "bright colors".

getsu, gatsu, tsuki

This pictographic character was modeled on the image of the waxing and waning moon.

月

Meaning moon, moonlight, month
This character is used as an element in compounds that are related to the moon, moonlight and time.
* Although they are identical in appearance, this character should not be confused with the abbreviated version of meat 肉 . (See p. 73.)

月日
(tsuki-hi)
time
**(gappi)*
date

			1	2	3	4
5	6	7	8	9	10	11
12	13	14	15	16	17	18
19	20	21	22	23	24	25
26	27	28	29	30	31	

月謝
(gessha)
monthly tuition

Since 謝 expresses appreciation, this compound indicates a monthly expression of appreciation.

満月
(man-getsu)
full moon
→三日月
(mi-ka-zuki)
new moon

月刊
(gekkan)
monthly periodical

→日刊
(nikkan)
daily newspaper or magazine

週刊
(shū-kan)
weekly magazine

満 means "full" and "complete".

刊 is related to "publishing" and "engraving".

有
(yū, u, a-ru)
to have

The element used in this kanji 月 is not derived from the moon, but is rather the abbreviation for meat 肉. It originally expressed "possession" and now means "to have", "to exist" and "to be". The opposite is 無, which expresses the negation of existance.

有頂天
(u-chō-ten)
ecstasy

有料
(yū-ryō)
payment required
←→ 無料
(mu-ryō)
free

有効
(yū-kō)
valid
←→ 無効
(mu-kō)
invalid

有効期限
20XX.

和服
(wa-fuku)
Japanese style dress

服
(fuku)
clothing

The original meaning of this kanji was "to compel someone to work". It is now also used in relation to "to swallow" and "clothing".

服役
(fuku-eki)
penal servitude

希望
(ki-bō)
hope

内服薬
(nai-fuku-yaku)
medicine taken internally

望
(bō, mō, nozo-mu)
to wish

From the original meaning of "full moon", this character was given the meanings of "to gaze out", "to hope for", and "desire".

眺望
(chō-bō)
view, prospect

期
(ki, go)
time

The original meaning of this character was one full cycle of the moon; "month". It was later adapted to mean "to meet", "to make an appointment", and "one year".

→ # 定期券
(tei-ki-ken)
a commuter pass

期待
(ki-tai)
expectation

半期
(han-ki)
half term, half a year
(same as 半年)
(han-toshi)

期年

賞味期限
(shō-mi-ki-gen)
expiration date for perishable food

朝
(chō, asa)
morning

From the original meaning of "sunrise", this kanji came to mean "morning". It is also used to denote imperial dynasties.

朝夕
(asa-yū)
morning and evening

朝市
(asa-ichi)
morning market

朝刊
(chō-kan)
morning edition

→ 夕刊
(yū-kan)
evening edition

The kanji for meat 肉 is abbreviated to a form that since the middle ages has come to be identical to the character for the moon; 月 . It is used in compounds that are related to parts of the body.

臓 means "organ" and is used in compounds for physical organs.

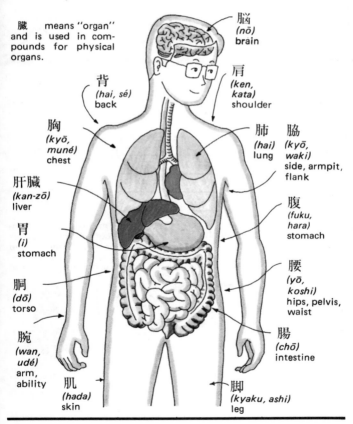

脳
(nō)
brain

肩
(ken, kata)
shoulder

背
(hai, sé)
back

胸
(kyō, muné)
chest

肺
(hai)
lung

脇
(kyō, waki)
side, armpit, flank

肝臓
(kan-zō)
liver

腹
(fuku, hara)
stomach

胃
(i)
stomach

腰
(yō, koshi)
hips, pelvis, waist

胴
(dō)
torso

腸
(chō)
intestine

腕
(wan, udé)
arm, ability

肌
(hada)
skin

脚
(kyaku, ashi)
leg

boku, moku, ki

This kanji is modeled after the image of a tree.

Meaning tree, wood

This character is used in compounds that are related to trees and things made from wood.

木材
(moku-zai)
lumber

材 means ingredient. This compound therefore indicates wood that is used for building things.
材木 *(zai-moku)* has the same meaning.

木綿
(mo-men)
cotton

The original meaning of this compound was "cotton plant". It later was used for cotton thread and cloth made from cotton. Its present use is generally for cotton cloth.

木曜日
(moku-yō-bi)
Thursday

→ 日曜日 *(nichi-yō-bi)*
   Sunday

   月曜日 *(getsu-yō-bi)*
   Monday

曜 is used for the days of the week. (See page 179.)

杉の木
(sugi-no-ki)
cryptomeria

This format is used to name kinds of trees.

本
(hon, moto)
source, book

The line through the lower part of the tree indicates its roots. The roots are the tree's source of nourishment. This led to the association of this character with "source", "origin", and "main part". When used as a prefix it means "correct" and "true". Since books were seen as the source of knowledge it came to mean "book".

日本
*(nippon *ni-hon)*
Japan

本店
(hon-ten)
head office

本名
(hon-myō)
real name

本屋
(hon-ya)
bookstore

BOOKSTORE

本当
(hon-tō)
true

really?

札
(satsu, fuda)
paper money, tag

Originally this character was used to mean bundles of bills tied together through holes in each of them. Later on it was used for each bill. It includes the meanings of "wooden tags", "paper money" and "religious wooden charms".

札束
(satsu-taba)
bundle of money

改札口
(kai-satsu-guchi)
ticket gate
(here 札 refers to a train ticket)

御札
(o-fuda)
charm, talisman
(o-satsu) money

未
(mi)
not yet

Modeled after the image of a tree with many branches, this kanji is used to mean "future", "still" and "not yet".

未成年
(mi-sei-nen)
underage

週末
(shū-matsu)
weekend

→ **月末**
(getsu-matsu)
the end of the month

年末
(nen-matsu)
the end of the year

MON
TUE
WED
THU
FRI
SAT
SUN

末
(ma-tsu, sué)
end

Although similar in design to the above kanji, this character has a line drawn across the top of a tree to indicate "end" and "last".

学校
(gakkō)
school

校
(kō)
school

The original design of this character includes a foot on a rail to indicate the idea of "leg irons". It was later used to mean "school", "to compare" and "to think".

〜様
(– sama)
Mr., Ms.

様
(yō, sama)
appearance

Created from the ancient word for "appearance" this character also means "manner", "circumstance" and "like or such as". Attached to names as a suffix it conveys respect for that person.

案
(an)
plan

This character was originally conceived of as a table on which to place cookware. It later came to mean "to think", "to worry" and "to propose".

案内所
(an-nai-jo)
information desk

瀬戸大橋
(sé-to-ō-hashi)
The Seto Ōhashi Bridge

橋
(kyō, hashi)
bridge

Originally this kanji meant "something tall and curved".

Here are some of the components that use 木 to express something related to trees.

桜
(ou, sakura)
cherry blossoms

梅
(bai, umé)
plum

林
(rin, hayashi)
woods

桑
(sō, kuwa)
mulberry

松
(shō, matsu)
pine

柿
(shi, kaki)
persimmon

栗
(ritsu, kuri)
chestnut

桃
(tō, momo)
peach

杉
(sugi)
cryptomeria

柳
(ryū, yanagi)
willow

森
(shin, mori)
forest

jo, nyo, onna

This character was drawn from the image of a woman seated with her hands held together.

女

Meaning woman

This kanji is used in compounds that are related to "woman", "feminity" and "blood relations".

男 *(dan, nan, otoko)* is the kanji used for "man".

女王
(jo-ō)
queen

→ 王女
(ō-jo)
princess

王 means king.

女房
(nyō-bō)
wife

In ancient times this compound meant a female official of the imperial court. Now this term is used by men to refer to their own wives. When referring to someone else's wife a more polite term 奥さん *(oku-san)* is used.

悪女
(aku-jo)
an evil, ugly woman

悪 means "bad" or "evil". In both the East and the West women were often associated with evil in ancient times. 妻 *(tsuma)* means wife and 悪妻 *(aku-sai)* means a bad wife. However, there is no compound which combines 悪 and 男.

女優
(jo-yū)
actress

優 means performer (see p. 64).

好
(kō, kono-mu, su-ku)
to like

The combination of a woman and a child 子 obviously refers to a young woman. As young woman are beautiful this character means "preference", "to like" and "good".

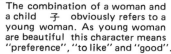

好物
(kō-butsu)
a favorite food

友好
(yū-kō)
friendship

好奇心
(kō-ki-shin)
curiosity

好都合
(kō-tsu-gō)
good circumstances

委
(i, yuda-neru)
to entrust

The original shape of this kanji was drawn to be slender and delicate. From the nuance of "delicate" came the idea of "to entrust".

婚約
(kon-yaku)
engagement

委員
(i-in)
people chosen to do work, a committee member

→ 委員会
(i-in-kai)
a committee

結婚
(kekkon)
marriage

← → 離婚
(ri-kon)
divorce

婚
(kon)
marriage

In ancient times marriage ceremonies began at dusk and continued through the night. The combination of a woman and an element that means "sunset" gave this kanji the meaning of "nuptial".

79

Here are some characters that use 女 to express something related to women.

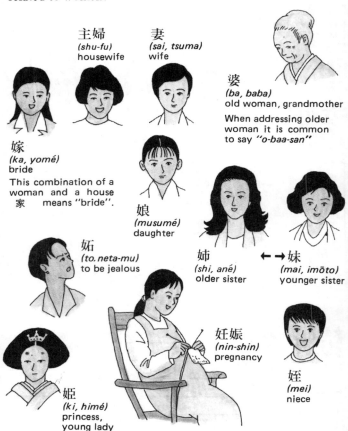

主婦
(shu-fu)
housewife

妻
(sai, tsuma)
wife

婆
(ba, baba)
old woman, grandmother

When addressing older woman it is common to say *"o-baa-san"*

嫁
(ka, yomé)
bride

This combination of a woman and a house 家 means "bride".

娘
(musumé)
daughter

妬
(to, neta-mu)
to be jealous

姉
(shi, ané)
older sister

←→

妹
(mai, imōto)
younger sister

妊娠
(nin-shin)
pregnancy

姫
(ki, himé)
princess, young lady

姪
(mei)
niece

始
(shi, haji-mé, haji-meru)
begin

All life begins with women. This character has a broader meaning of "to start" and "to commence".
終 *(shū, o-waru)* is an antonym which means "to finish".
初 has the same *kun* reading as 始 ; "haji-mé". However the former conveys the idea of "the beginning", "initial part", whereas the latter means "to begin a process".

開始
(kai-shi)
to commence

年始
(nen-shi)
the beginning of the year

始末
(shi-matsu)
to finish, to settle

←→ 年末
(nen-matsu)
the end of the year

姿
(shi, sugata)
physical appearance

Originally this character expressed a person's natural appearance but is now also used for one's gestures, apparel and overall appearance.

姿勢
(shi-sei)
posture

嫌煙権
(ken-en-ken)
the right to be free from other's cigarette smoke

嫌
(ken, gen, kira-u)
to hate

This character is used to express light distaste as well as strong hatred and suspicion.

機嫌
(ki-gen)
feeling

MY NAME IS...

姓名
(sei-mei)
full name

姓
(sei, shō)
family name

This character combines a woman with life 生 to indicate a blood relation.

81

sha, kuruma

With a center portion carried by two axles, this character represents a cart or other vehicle.

車

Meaning wheeled vehicle (cart, car, truck, train etc.)
This kanji is used in compounds that are related to vehicles.

車輪
(sha-rin)
wheel

輪 is used for "ring", "circle" and other round objects.

車座
(kuruma-za)
to sit in a circle

座 means to sit.

乗車
(jō-sha)
to get on (a vehicle)

乗る *(no-ru)* is drawn from the image of a person who has climbed up a tree. It means "to ride".

風車
(kaza-guruma)
wind-propelled toy
* *(hū-sha)* windmill

軍
(gun)
military

This kanji was derived from which means to surround and "car". The car is a tank and so this character has the meanings of "army" and "military".

軍備
(gun-bi)
armament

運転
(un-ten)
to drive or operate a machine

転入
(ten-nyū)
to move in

←→転出
(ten-shutsu)
to move out

転
(ten, koro-bu)
to turn

Based on the idea of a spinning wheel, this kanji expresses the ideas of "to turn", "to remove", "to change", "to go around" and "to roll".

軽
(kei, karu-i)
light

Originally modeled after an empty cart, this character means "light", "easy", "to make light of", "thin" and "uneasy".

軽重
(kei-jū, *kei-chō)
light and heavy, importance

軽蔑
(kei-betsu)
scorn

輸血
(yu-ketsu)
blood transfusion

輸入
(yu-nyū)
import

←→輸出
(yu-shutsu)
export

輸
(yu)
to transport

The original meaning of this character was to move. It later was extended to "to transport" and "to ship".

83

Sights Around Town

車道
(sha-dō)
road

歩道
(ho-dō)
walkway

軽自動車
(kei-ji-dō-sha)
light weight automobile

駐車場
(chū-sha-jō)
parking lot

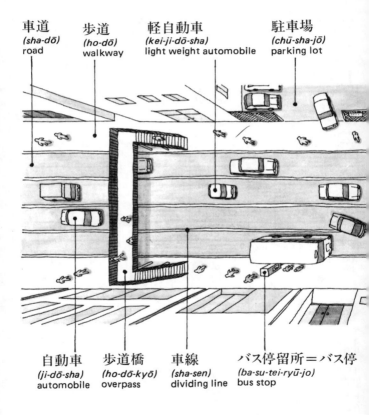

自動車
(ji-dō-sha)
automobile

歩道橋
(ho-dō-kyō)
overpass

車線
(sha-sen)
dividing line

バス停留所＝バス停
(ba-su-tei-ryū-jo)
bus stop

赤信号 ←→ 青信号
(aka-shin-gō)   *(ao-shin-gō)*
red light   green light

二輪車   交差点   横断歩道
(ni-rin-sha)   *(kō-sa-ten)*   *(ō-dan-ho-dō)*
two wheeled vehicle   intersection   pedestrian crosswalk

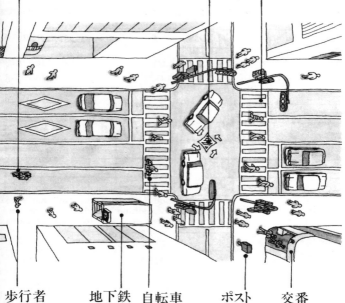

歩行者   地下鉄   自転車   ポスト   交番
(ho-kō-sha)   *(chi-ka-tetsu)*   *(ji-ten-sha)*   *(po-su-to)*   *(kō-ban)*
pedestrian   subway   bicycle   mailbox   police box

shu, té

This pictographic character was modeled after the image of a hand with five fingers extended.

Meaning hand, palm, to hold, to lend a hand, method, used to refer to a talented technician

The abbreviated form of this character 扌 is called *"tehen"*. It is used in compounds that are related to hands or something performed with the hands.

手紙
(té-gami)
letter

A letter is something that is written by hand.

手入れ
(té-i-ré)
to work on,
to care for

The basic meaning of this compound is to apply one's hands to something in order to improve it. It is also used to mean "to catch a criminal".

手間
(té-ma)
time, labor

Since 間 means time, this compound conveys the idea of "time needed to perform something".

握手
(aku-shu)
handshake

握 means to grasp firmly. Rather than shake hands when they meet, Japanese usually bow to each other. However, they do often wave good-bye.

打
(da, u-tsu)
to hit

This character conveys the basic meanings of "to hit" and "to stroke". It is sometimes attached as a suffix with no meaning.

打撃
(da-geki)
to strike and attack, damage

打ち消し
(u-chi-ké-shi)
denial, negation

打ち水
(u-chi-mizu)
to sprinkle water to clean or cool off something

打診
(da-shin)
to examine a body by tapping, percussion, to sound someone out about something

払
(hutsu, hara-u)
to pay

This character is used for many actions performed by the hand: "to wipe", "to brush", "to knock over" and "to pay".

支払い
(shi-hara-i)
to make a payment

払い戻し
(hara-i-modo-shi)
to pay back

招待状
(shō-tai-jō)
invitation

招
(shō, mané-ku)
to invite

Derived from the notion of "to call", this kanji expresses "calling attention with the hands" and "to invite".

挙
(kyo, a-geru)
to raise

Originally this character meant "to pick up with the hands". It is now used to express "to hold with the hand", "to raise high", "to throw a party", "to give an example" and "to line up".

技術
(gi-jutsu)
technique

選挙
(sen-kyo)
election

快挙
(kai-kyo)
splendid achievement

技
(gi, waza)
technique

From the original meaning of "to work", this kanji has come to mean "skill" and "ability".

寝技
(né-waza)
pinning techniques in *jūdō* and wrestling

扱
(atsuka-u)
to treat

From the original meaning of "to control with the hands", this kanji has come to mean "to treat" and "to deal with".

取り扱い
(to-ri-atsuka-i)
handling

折り紙
(o-ri-gami)
origami, the art of folding paper

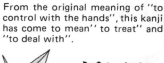

骨折
(kossetsu)
to break a bone

折
(setsu, o-ru)
to fold, to bend

The combination of a *tehen* and an ax 斤 expresses the process of a tree being cut down. From this came the meanings of "to bend", "to sprain" and "to crush". This character is also used for "time" and "candy boxes".

菓子折
(ka-shi-ori)
candy box

投
(tō, na-geru)
to throw

The combination of a *tehen* and an element meaning "careless" produces this kanji's meanings of "to toss", "to throw away", "to stop" and "to take advantage of".

投票
(tō-hyō)
to vote

投書
(tō-sho)
to write a letter to a newspaper

投手
(tō-shu)
baseball pitcher

押
(ō, o-su, osa-eru)
to push

Originally this kanji meant "to restrain". It is now used for "to hold down", "to push closed" "to stamp" and other similar actions.

押し問答
(o-shi-mon-dō)
to bandy with words

押印
(ō-in)
to stamp a seal

振
(shin, fu-ru)
to shake

The basic meaning of this is "to shake" and "to move". It also means "to brandish", "to excite", "to assign", "to hold" and "to deceive".

不振
(fu-shin)
economic slump, unsatisfactory

振動
(shin-dō)
vibration

振り込み
(fu-ri-ko-mi)
to transfer money to an account

持
(ji, mo-tsu)
to hold

The original meaning of this character was to restrain something with the hands. Later it took on the meaning of "to move with the hands", "to take", "to hold", "to maintain" and "to possess".

→ **持ち物**
(mo-chi-mono)
belongings

持病
(ji-byō)
chronic disease

拾得物
(shū-toku-butsu)
found article

拾
(shū, jū, hiro-u)
to find

Originally this kanji meant "to take in one after another". It is now used for "to find", "to pick up" and "to hold down with both hands".

捨て身
(su-té-mi)
to risk one's life for something

捨
(sha, su-teru)
to throw away

Derived from the idea of "to remove with the hands", this character is used for "to throw away" and "to leave as is".

採
(sai, to-ru)
to take

The original concept for this character was a finger cutting a plant's bud. From this it developed to include "to cut", "to take out" and "to select".

採集
(sai-shū)
to collect

排水
(hai-sui)
drainage

排
(hai)
exhaust

The combination of a *tehen* and 非 ("contrary", "to remove") gives this character the meaning of "to push open", "to push out", "to reject" and "exhaust".

指
(shi, yubi, sa-su)
finger

This character originally meant "to separate". It indicates the separated parts of a hand; the fingers. It also means "to point to" and "to indicate".

指切り
(yubi-ki-ri)
In a sign of good faith when making a promise, two people wrap their little fingers around each other to signify a bond.

指名
(shi-mei)
to nominate, to designate

屈指
(kusshi)
outstanding (something so good that one uses his fingers to emphasize its excellence)

指紋
(shi-mon)
fingerprint

The Names of the Fingers

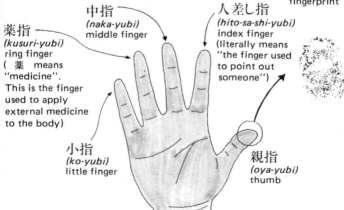

薬指
(kusuri-yubi)
ring finger
(薬 means "medicine".
This is the finger used to apply external medicine to the body)

中指
(naka-yubi)
middle finger

人差し指
(hito-sa-shi-yubi)
index finger
(literally means "the finger used to point out someone")

小指
(ko-yubi)
little finger

親指
(oya-yubi)
thumb

shi, ito

糸

This pictographic character was modeled on the image of several strands of raw silk protruding from a cocoon. These are wrapped together to form a single thread.

Meaning thread, threadlike substances, a minute amount
This character is used in compounds that signify "intertwined relationships".

毛糸
(ké-ito)
wool yarn

毛 means hair. In this case it means "wool". This compound is used for all knitting threads.

糸口
(ito-guchi)
the end of a thread, a lead, a clue

製糸
(sei-shi)
to spin thread

製 was formed from the idea of cutting cloth to make clothing. It means "to manufacture".

抜糸
(basshi)
to remove stitches from a wound

抜 means "to pull out".

級
(kyū)
rank

The original meaning of this character was "to continue in order". It referred to continuous stitching when sewing cloth. From there it came to mean "level", "class", "position" and "status".

進級
(shin-kyū)
to move on to a higher grade

高級品
(kō-kyū-hin)
luxury items

口紅
(kuchi-beni)
lipstick

紅
(kō, ku, kurenai, beni, aka-i)
red

This kanji expresses the color of dyed thread. It is used for bright colors, red cosmetics made from safflower and lipsticks.

紅葉
(kō-yō)
the changing of the leaves in the fall

真紅
(shin-ku)
crimson

紅茶
(kō-cha)
black tea

紫陽花
(ajisai)
hydrangea

紫外線
(shi-gai-sen)
ultraviolet rays

紫
(shi, murasaki)
purple

This kanji originally indicated the shade of purple used in textiles. It is now used for "purple" in general. It is also sometimes used in an affected manner to call "soy sauce".

約 *(yaku)* vow

The process of attaching something tightly with a rope is akin to this kanji's meanings of "to resume", "to simplify", "approximately", "to swear" and "to refrain".

約束 *(yaku-soku)* promise

節約 *(setsu-yaku)* to conserve

約1万円 *(yaku-ichi-man-en)* approximately 10,000 yen.

紙幣 *(shi-hei)* paper money

表紙 *(hyō-shi)* cover page

紙 *(shi, kami)* paper

Although this character is now used to mean "paper", it was originally conceived of as "a smooth silk cloth".

素顔 *(su-gao)* a natural face

素 *(so, su, moto)* element

The original idea for this kanji was "white thread". The purity of a white thread led to this character's use to mean "source", "element" and "pure".

素人 *(shirōto)* amateur

質素 *(shisso)* simple, frugal

経験
(kei-ken)
experience

経
(kei, kyō, hé-ru, ta-tsu)
longitude

This character originally stood for a vertical thread being stretched straight during weaving. It then took on the meanings of "straight thread", "order", "to pass", "reason", "to control" and "to manage".

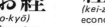
お経
(o-kyō)
the sutras

経済
(kei-zai)
economy

経緯
(kei-i)
longitude and latitude, details

終点
(shū-ten)
terminal

終
(shū, o-waru)
to finish

When one finishes sewing he ties a knot at the end of the thread. This kanji was originally used to describe this process. Later on it came to mean "finish", "to end" "to complete" and "at last".

最終回
(sai-shū-kai)
last inning

終日
(shū-jitsu)
all day

番組
(ban-gumi)
television program

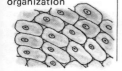
組織
(so-shiki)
organization

組
(so, ku-mu)
group

The original meaning is to wind thread by hand. From there it came to mean "assemble", "group" and "set".

絵
(kai, é)
picture

This kanji originally meant "to combine five colors". It now includes "colored pictures", "drawings" and "sketches".

油絵
(abura-é)
oil painting

結納
(yui-nō)
engagement presents

結果
(kekka)
result

結
(ketsu, musu-bu, yu-u)
to connect

The original meaning of this character was "to bend". This led to the idea of creating a knot with thread in order to tie things together. From here came its uses as "to bind", "to complete" and "to shut".

綿
(men, wata)
cotton

Originally used to describe the process of attaching threads to create silk clothes, this kanji now means "cotton", "to join" and "small".

綿毛
(wata-gé)
down, fuzz

緊急
(kin-kyū)
emergency

119

緊
(kin)
tight

This kanji's original meaning of "to wind thread tightly" was later expanded to include "to shut tightly", "strict", "urgent" and "to condense".

停止線
(tei-shi-sen)
stop line

← **線**
(sen)
line

Originally used to mean "thin thread", this character now means "line". It is used for train lines as well.

→ **山手線**
(yama-no-té-sen)
the Yamanoté Line train

細
(sai, hoso-i, koma-kai)
thin

This kanji originally meant "extremely small" and referred to a narrow thread. It now expresses "thin", "minute", "detailed", "thorough" and "few".

→ **細菌**
(sai-kin)
microbe

細工
(sai-ku)
craftmanship

縦横
(jū-ō)
vertical and horizontal, to control at will

縦
(jū, taté)
height

The original meaning was related to the act of releasing a tightly pulled thread. From there it expanded to include "loose", "self-indulgence", "to release" and "vertical".

総理大臣
(sō-ri-dai-jin)
Prime Minister

総
(sō)
whole

This character evolved from the process of collecting threads and binding them together. It now means "to comprise", "to control" and "total".

kin, kon, kané

The original meaning of this character was "to shine". It was modeled after two shining points.

Meaning metal, mineral, gold, money, metallic objects

The composition of something shiny inside the earth 土 led to this kanji's meanings of "mineral". It is also used for "Friday". It is included in compounds that are related to metal.

金利
(kin-ri)
interest

利 means "profit". So 金利 is profit made from money; interest.

現金
(gen-kin)
cash

現 means to appear on the surface. So, 現金 is money that one has at hand for immediate use.

金髪
(kin-patsu)
blond

髪 means "hair". In this case 金 is gold, so this compound means "golden hair".

お金
(o-kané)
money

This is the most common word used to refer to money.

針
(shin, hari)
needle

This kanji is used for many long metallic objects including "needle", "pin", "hook" and "watch hand".

まち針
(ma-chi-bari)
marking pin

針山
(hari-yama)
pin cushion

針路
(shin-ro)
course, direction

鉄道
(tetsu-dō)
railroad

鉄則
(tessoku)
an ironclad rule

鉄
(tetsu)
iron

From the original meaning of "reddish black", this kanji took on the meaning of "rusted iron". It is also used for black objects, weapons, and hard objects.

鉄火巻
(tekka-maki)
A *sushi* roll made with raw tuna

風鈴
(fū-rin)
wind chime

鈴蘭
(suzu-ran)
lily-of-the-valley

鈴
(rei, rin, suzu)
bell

Although this character originally meant "the ringing of a bell", it is now used to express the bell itself.

銀
(gin)
silver

From the original meaning of "white", this character took on the meaning of "white metal". It later was used for "silver", "silvery metals" and "silver coins".

銀行
(gin-kō)
bank

銀盤
(gin-ban)
silver plate, poetic word for an ice skating rink

銀世界
(gin-sé-kai)
an area covered with snow

銅像
(dō-zō)
bronze statue

銅
(dō)
copper

Derived from the word "red", this character is used for "red metal"; copper.

鋭利
(ei-ri)
keenness

鋭
(ei, surudo-i)
sharp

Derived from a word meaning "the long thin part of a weapon", this character means "sharp", "pointed", "clever" and "knowledgeable".

小銭
(ko-zeni)
small change

銭
(sen, zeni)
money

This character was originally used to describe "thin metallic edges of farming instruments". Since ancient money resembled this shape, this kanji came to mean "money".

錦鯉
(nishiki-goi)
colored carp

錦
(kin, nishiki)
brocade

Derived from a shining image, this character is used for fancy embroidered cloth and other similarly beautiful objects.

合鍵
(ai-kagi)
spare key

鍵
(ken, kagi)
key

Derived from the notion of "to close", this character is now used for all sorts of keys, including keys on a piano.

双眼鏡
(sō-gan-kyō)
binoculars

鏡
(kyō, kagami)
mirror

Derived from the ancient word for "to see", this character now means "mirror". The 金 in this character's composition is due to the fact that in the past, mirrors were made from metal. It is now also used to mean "glasses".

閉鎖
(hei-sa)
to shut down

鎖
(sa, kusari)
chain

The original meaning of this character was "to close firmly". This led to its use for "chain" and "connection".

土鍋
(do-nabé)
earthenware pot

鍋
(ka, nabé)
pan, pot

The original meaning of this character was "to mix". A pan is used to mix many foods while cooking.

kō, ku, kuchi

This pictographic character was derived from a drawing of a mouth.

口

Meaning mouth, person, entrance, food, edge, beginning, variety, job

This character is used in compounds that are related to the mouth, sounds, and language.

非常口
(hi-jō-guchi)
emergency exit

非常 means emergency.

窓口
(mado-guchi)
window

窓 simply means "window". When combined here with 口 they mean "ticket window", "cashier window" or "contact".

口座
(kō-za)
account

The original meaning of this compound was to calculate by recording things under different classifications. It is used for all kinds of financial bank accounts.

悪口
(waru-kuchi)
to slander

In this case 口 means a person, so this compound means "to bad-mouth someone".

可
(ka)
good

Derived from the idea of "good", this character indicates "approval". It is also used to mean "to have no problems", "advantage", "to allow" and "possibility".

可能
(ka-nō)
possible

←→ 不可能
(fu-ka-nō)
impossible

許可
(kyo-ka)
permission

古書
(ko-sho)
ancient writings

古
(ko, furu-i)
old

The combination of 口 and ten 十 involves the process of transmitting information about the older generation. After ten repetitions the information becomes very old. This kanji conveys "old", "ancient" and "the past". It is the opposite of 今 (see p. 61).

古都
(ko-to)
ancient capital

考古学
(kō-ko-gaku)
archaeology

のぞみ号
(no-zo-mi-gō)
the name of a Shinkansen between Tokyo and Fukuoka

号泣
(gō-kyū)
lamentation

号
(gō)
number

This kanji originally meant "to cry out sadly". From there it expanded to include "to weep", "to scream", "to shout out", "life", "common name", "seal" and "store name".

台
(tai, dai)
stand

The original meaning was a high building used to see far away or an artificially constructed hill. Later it came to mean "to elevate", "to support", "tower" and "foundation".

台所
(dai-dokoro)
kitchen

台風
(tai-fū)
typhoon

舞台
(bu-tai)
stage

各地
(kaku-chi)
each place

各
(kaku, ono-ono)
each

The original meaning of this kanji was "to have a different opinion". This led to its use as "individual", "each" and "many".

各種
(kaku-shu)
all types

大吉
(dai-kichi)
good fortune
←→凶
(kyō)
misfortune

吉報
(kippō)
good news

吉
(kichi)
good luck

Originally used as a prayer word, this character now means "fortune", "congratulations" and "joy".

方向
(hō-kō)
direction

向
(kō, mu-ku)
to face

The original meaning of this kanji was a high window on the northern side of a house. From that it came to mean "to look straight forward", "to be bound for" and "to suit".

向日葵
(himawari)
sunflower

A sunflower faces the sun and follows it through the sky. For this reason it was written with these characters.

合
(gō, a-u)
to fit

The original meaning of this character was "to respond to someone". It later expanded to include "to join", "to match", "to gather", "to exchange" and "to moderate". In the traditional Japanese system of weights and measures 一合 *(ichi-gō)* equals 0.18 liters. This character is still used to count cups of *saké* and rice.

合格
(gō-kaku)
to pass a test

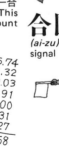

合図
(ai-zu)
signal

同時
(dō-ji)
simultaneously

合計
(gō-kei)
total

```
      5.74
      1.32
      9.03
      7.91
      8.00
      7.31
      5.27
TOTAL 44.58
```

同行
(dō-kō)
to go together

同
(dō, ona-ji)
same

This kanji originally meant "to call many people together". From this it came to mean "a crowd of people", "colleague", "similar", "equal" and "to line up".

名

(mei, myō, na)
name

This compound is made from a mouth and the character for evening 夕 . Once night falls and visibility is diminished it becomes necessary to identify oneself to others encountered on the road. This led to the meaning of "name", "to give a name" and "honor". This character is used as a unit for counting people.

名前
(na-maé)
name

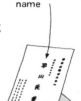

名作
(mei-saku)
masterpiece

名刺
(mei-shi)
name card

君
(kun, kimi)
Mr., you

The original meaning of this character was "a person who gives orders"; a ruler. It is attached as a prefix to names when a person of high social ranking refers respectfully to someone of a lower status or when good friends talk to each other.

〜君
(-kun)
Mr.

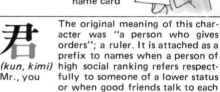

Mr.

告白
(koku-haku)
confession

告
(koku,
tsugé-ru)
to inform

The original composition of this character contained a word that was moving upward. This conveyed "to give advice to someone". Later it came to mean "to tell", "to inform", "to indicate" and "to inquire".

告別式
(koku-betsu-shiki)
funeral service

告知板
(koku-chi-ban)
bulletin board

広告
(kō-koku)
advertisement

塩味
(shio-aji)
salty

味
(mi, aji)
taste

The basic meaning of this character is "delicious". It is also used for "to experience", "taste", "flavor" and "feeling".

味噌
(mi-so)
fermented bean paste

味方
(mi-kata)
ally

意味
(i-mi)
meaning

命
(mei, myō, inochi)
life

Derived from the idea of "teachings", this character originally meant "the word of god". It has come to mean "life", "command", "rules" and "destiny".

生命
(sei-mei)
life

和食
(wa-shoku)
Japanese style cooking

和
(wa, yawa-ragu)
peace

The original design of this character involved the idea of "responding to someone's voice". From this came the ideas of "harmonic unity", "calm", "peace" and "to soothe". This character also means "Japan".

和解
(wa-kai)
reconciliation

英和辞典
(ei-wa-ji-ten)
an English-Japanese dictionary
英 means England or English. (see p. 65)

品
(hin, shina)
goods

The combination of three mouths means "many things". This character refers to the quality of individual objects.

品質
(hin-shitsu)
quality

気品
(ki-hin)
refinement

粗品
(so-shina)
free promotional samples

粗 means "rough" and "crude". As a sign of humility, Japanese describe a gift that they are giving as a very insignificant, unimportant, inexpensive item. This is only an expression of humility and has no bearing at all on the gift.

商
(shō, akina-u)
to trade

This character was originally used to mean "a travelling salesman". It now is used in a wider sense for "trade" and "commerce".

小売商
(ko-uri-shō)
retail trade

商人
(shō-nin)
merchant

商品
(shō-hin)
sales item

商店
(shō-ten)
store

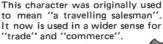

訪問
(hō-mon)
to visit

問
(mon, to-u)
to ask

The original meaning of "to listen and inquire" has essentially remained intact in this character which means "to ask", "to question", "to research" and "to discuss".

問い合わせ
(to-i-a-wa-sé)
inquiry

問題
(mon-dai)
problem, issue

喫茶店
(kissa-ten)
coffee shop

喫
(kitsu)
to eat

Originally this kanji meant only "to eat", but it has taken on the meanings of "to drink" and "to smoke" as well.

喫煙所
(kitsu-en-jo)
smoking area

善意
(zen-i)
good will

←→ **悪意**
(aku-i)
malice

善
(zen, yo-i)
good, virtuous

Originally this character meant "great fortune". It now includes "good", "skilled", "reasonable", "moral" and "virtuous".

単
(tan)
single, one

The original design of this character 單 included two mouths.

単位
(tan-i)
unit

単3乾電池
(tan-san-kan-den-chi)
AA size battery

単行本
(tan-kō-bon)
separate volume

器用
(ki-yō)
dexterous

楽器
(gakki)
musical instrument

器
(ki, utsuwa)
vessel

The original character was composed of several mouths and a dog 犬 to convey the idea of "many barking dogs". Later on it came to mean "cooking ware", "utensil" "useful item", "work" and "ability".

Actions Performed With the Mouth

In some cases two or more kanji mean the same thing.

呼ぶ
(yo-bu)
to call

叫ぶ
(saké-bu)
to scream

吸う
(su-u)
to smoke

吹く
(fu-ku)
to blow

叱る
(shika-ru)
to scold

鳴く
(na-ku)
to cry,
to bark,
to yelp

呑む
(no-mu)
to swallow

呻く
(umē-ku)
to groan

咳
(seki)
cough

嚙む
(ka-mu)
to chew

唸る
(una-ru)
to growl

吐く
(ha-ku)
to vomit

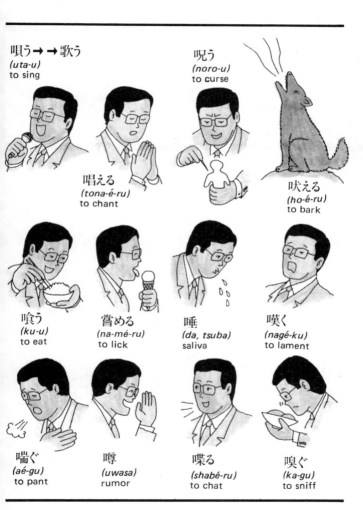

唄う➡➡歌う
(uta-u)
to sing

呪う
(noro-u)
to curse

唱える
(tona-é-ru)
to chant

吠える
(ho-é-ru)
to bark

喰う
(ku-u)
to eat

嘗める
(na-mé-ru)
to lick

唾
(da, tsuba)
saliva

嘆く
(nagé-ku)
to lament

喘ぐ
(aé-gu)
to pant

噂
(uwasa)
rumor

喋る
(shabé-ru)
to chat

嗅ぐ
(ka-gu)
to sniff

(kunigamaé)

This is the original form of the characters 囲 "to enclose" and 国 "nation". It is no longer used as an independent character except as an abbreviation for 国 .

Meaning to enclose, to circle around

Despite its resemblance to the character for mouth, this is a different character. It is called "*kunigamaé*". This element is used in ideographic compounds that are often abstractly related to the idea of "to enclose".

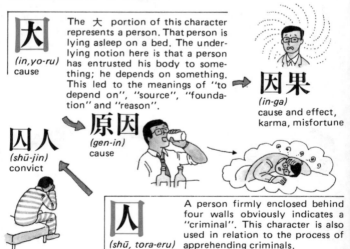

因
(in, yo-ru)
cause

The 大 portion of this character represents a person. That person is lying asleep on a bed. The underlying notion here is that a person has entrusted his body to something; he depends on something. This led to the meanings of "to depend on", "source", "foundation" and "reason".

因果
(in-ga)
cause and effect, karma, misfortune

原因
(gen-in)
cause

囚人
(shū-jin)
convict

囚
(shū, tora-eru)
criminal

A person firmly enclosed behind four walls obviously indicates a "criminal". This character is also used in relation to the process of apprehending criminals.

回
(kai, é, mawa-su)
turn

The combination of a large and a small version of this element expresses "different extremes". It is used to mean "to rotate", "to circle around", "to return" and "curved". It is also used as a counter for repeated actions.

→ **回転**
(kai-ten)
rotation

回覧
(kai-ran)
to circulate
(a memo etc...)

回数
(kai-sū)
times

→ 1回   2回……
(ikkai)   *(ni-kai)*
once   twice

一 → 丁

正正
正丁

囲碁
(i-go)
go (an Oriental
game of strategy)

囲
(i, kako-mu)
to surround

The enclosed character originally meant "to patrol". Later on this compound came to mean "to enclose", "to encircle" and "to go around".

周囲
(shū-i)
surrounding area

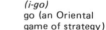

困難
(kon-nan)
difficult

貧困
(hin-kon)
poverty

困
(kon, koma-ru)
to have trouble

The tree contained in this enclosure faces great difficulties in growing; thus this character's meanings of "to be difficult" and "to have trouble with". Another explanation for this character is that of a tree taking root around a house and causing problems. This led to the meanings of "to suffer", "to tire" and "poor".

113

図
(to, zu, haka-ru)
plan

The original form of this character contained a grain field being harvested and the surrounding area. It meant "map". This led to the meanings of "to measure", "to consult", "to plot", "to sketch" and "drawing".

➡ **地図**
(chi-zu)
map

図書館
(to-sho-kan)
library

図星
(zu-boshi)
bull's eye

頑固
(gan-ko)
stubborn

固形
(ko-kei)
solid

古
(ko, kata-meru)
hard

The outer enclosure is symbolic of the walls that surrounded ancient capitals. The inner portion means "hard". This combination originally meant "to defend", but it is now used to mean "hard", "to set" and "to fortify".

国
(koku, kuni)
nation

The original inspiration for this character was "an area with a border constructed around it". This led to the meanings of "nation", "state" and "hometown".

外国
(gai-koku)
foreign nation

国立〜
(koku-ritsu)
national

国会
(kokkai)
parliament

国立博物

円盤
(en-ban)
disk

圓 ⇨ 円
(en)
circle, yen

The ancient form of this kanji expressed the idea of "round". This gave rise to the meanings "to go smoothly", "to be full", "surrounding area" and "circle". This is the character used for the yen, the Japanese currency.

円周率
(en-shū-ritsu)
pi

πr^2

$2\pi r$

円高
(en-daka)
a strong yen rate

園
(en, sono)
garden

Although this kanji was devised for the limited meaning of "fruit tree" and "garden", it now includes "vegetable", "flower field" and more complicated meanings such as "to show something to someone", "to enjoy" and "to educate and take care of children".

公園
(kō-en)
park

園芸
(en-gei)
botany

保育園
(ho-iku-en)
kindergarten

動物園
(dō-butsu-en)
zoo

開園
(kai-en)
to open a park

← → 閉園
(hei-en)
to close a park

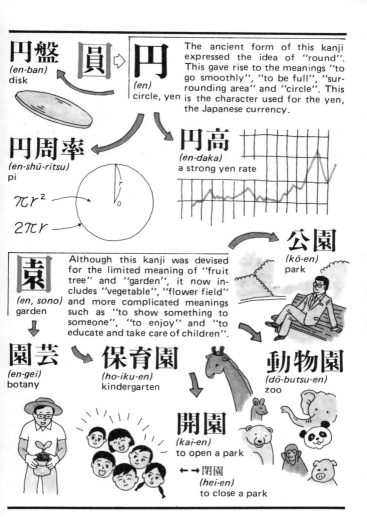

gen, gon, i-u, koto

This character evolved from the ancient idea for "spirit", "thought" and "mind". The design shows a spirit coming out of a mouth.

言

舌 ▷ 舌 ▷ 舌 ▷ 言

Meaning   word, to speak, to express one's feelings

The underlying idea is that a person's voice is the expression of his or her inner thoughts. When used in compounds this character is called a *"gonben"*. It is used in relation to the process of communication.

言動
(gen-dō)
words and deeds

動 means "to move" or "to do".

予言
(yo-gen)
prediction

予 is a prefix that means "pre" and "before". This combination involves the process of speaking in advance; predicting.

言い訳
(i-i-waké)
excuse

Since 訳 means "reason", this compound means words spoken to justify something; usually improper behaviour.

伝言板
(den-gon-ban)
message board

伝 means to transmit. The combination of 伝 and 言 means "message". 板 means "board". 伝言板 are located at train stations and airports for use in contacting travelers.

116

計
(kei, haka-ru)
to measure

The original meaning of this character was "to collect". Part of the collecting process is keeping track of what and how many items have been collected. This involves "counting" and "measuring". From here came the meanings "to calculate", "to gauge", "to estimate" and "to plan".

計画
(kei-kaku)
a plan

会計
(kai-kei)
account, bill

体温計
(tai-on-kei)
thermometer

記録
(ki-roku)
record

記
(ki, shiru-su)
to write down

This character was initially used to mean "a written recording". From there it came to mean "to learn", "to record", "to remember" and "to describe".

記念写真
(ki-nen-sha-shin)
commemorative photograph

記事
(ki-ji)
newspaper or magazine article

記憶
(ki-oku)
memory

MEMORY

速記
(sokki)
stenography

許
(kyo, yuru-su)
to permit

From an initial meaning of "to agree with someone", this character took on the meanings of "to allow", "to permit" and "to forgive". ➤

許可
(kyo-ka)
permission

運転免許証
(un-ten-men-kyo-shō)
driver's license
(often abbreviated as 免許)

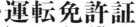

通訳
(tsū-yaku)
interpretation

訳
(yaku, waké)
translation

The fundamental meaning of this kanji is "to change". Specifically it is used for "changing words"; translation. It also means "reason", "excuse" and "cause".

翻訳
(hon-yaku)
written translation

翻訳
TRANSLATION

学生証
(gaku-sei-shō)
student I.D. card

証
(shō, akashi)
proof

This character's original meanings of "to inform" and "to admonish" have given way in modern times to the meanings "to prove", "evidence", "to certify" and "to witness".

証人
(shō-nin)
witness

証券会社
(shō-ken-gai-sha)
securities firm

保証書
(ho-shō-sho)
warranty certificate

保証書

英会話
(ei-kai-wa)
English conversation

話
(wa, hana-su, hanashi)
to talk

Originally this character was used for things that had been passed down verbally from one generation to another. Such things were considered valuable and instructive. This kanji now means "to talk".

昔話
(mukashi-banashi)
fairy tale
(昔 means the past)

Once upon a time...

世話
(sé-wa)
to look after

語
(go, kata-ru)
to tell,
to narrate

Derived from the idea for "mutual", this character was given the meaning of "to exchange words". It now means "to recite", "to narrate", "to tell" and "to inform".

語尾
(go-bi)
the end of a word, a suffix

物語
(mono-gatari)
tale

外国語
(gai-koku-go)
foreign language
→ 英語 *(ei-go)* English
仏語 *(futsu-go)* French

落語
(raku-go)
comic story

誤解
(go-kai)
misunderstand

誤
(go, ayama-ru, ayama-ri)
to err

From its original meaning of "to exaggerate", this character came to mean "to be mistaken", "to mislead", "to blunder" and "accidental".

正	誤
ただしい ←	ただしく
to err ←	to eer

正誤表
(sei-go-hyō)
errata

119

読
(doku, toku, yo-mu)
to read

The original meaning of this kanji was "to read aloud". It evolved to include "to read in an affected manner", "to perceive", "to understand" and "pronunciation".

読書
(doku-sho)
to read a book

読者
(doku-sha)
reader

愛読書
(ai-doku-sho)
favorite book

試
(shi, kokoro-miru)
to test

This character was first used to mean "to taste a new food". This later expanded to include "to try", "to attempt" and "to test".

試合
(shi-ai)
sports match

試写会
(shi-sha-kai)
film preview

入学試験
(nyū-gaku-shi-ken)
school entrance examination
(abbreviated to 入試)

日課
(nikka)
daily workload

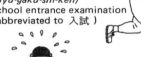

課
(ka)
lesson, section

This character originally meant "to consider" and "to test". These meanings were extended to include "to attempt", "to assign work", "to levy a tax" and "to divide".

課税
(ka-zei)
tax assessment

課長
(ka-chō)
section chief

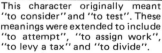

診療所
(shin-ryō-jo)
clinic

診
(shin, mi-ru)
to examine

In this character the original meaning of "to look at" has come to mean "physical examination" and "to diagnose".

診断書
(shin-dan-sho)
medical certificate

誕
(tan)
to be born

This character was derived from the idea of "to draw out". It is mainly used for "birth", but also contains the meanings of "to exaggerate", "to postpone" and "to deceive".

誕生日
(tan-jō-bi)
birthday

感謝
(kan-sha)
appreciation

謝
(sha, ayama-ru)
to apologize

Derived from the notion of "to interrupt", this character first meant "to refuse" and "farewell greeting". This led to the modern meanings of "to apologize" and "to express gratitude".

謝罪
(sha-zai)
to apologize

警
(kei)
to admonish

This character was based on the idea of "to reprove". It now means "to warn", "caution" and "to protect".

警察
(kei-satsu)
police

婦警
(fu-kei)
policewoman

to, do, tsuchi

The bottom line of this character represents the earth and the upper portion conveys a prayer dedicated to nature's ability to make things grow.

Meaning   ground, nation, Saturday

This character is used in compounds related to the earth and soil.

土台
(do-dai)
foundation

This compound is used for both abstract and concrete nuances; "building foundations" as well as "the essence of things".

土用
(do-yō)
midsummer

This compound represents the first 18 days of each season as measured by the ancient Japanese calendar. It is used especially for the beginning of summer, a time when it is customary to eat eel because it is said to be nutritious and fortifying against the summer heat.

土足
(do-soku)
while wearing shoes

The combination of earth and foot 足 obviously means dirty feet. This refers to a person who is wearing outdoor footwear. In Japanese houses and traditional restaurants it is customary to remove all shoes worn outside before entering a room.

土産
(miyagé)
souvenir

The combination of earth and a character that means "produce" 産 indicates "locally produced products". This is now used to mean souvenir presents that people bring home from vacation.

在
(zai, a-ru)
to exist

The original meaning was "something found in the ground". This was extended to mean "to be", "to have" and "to exist".

自由自在
(ji-yū-ji-zai)
at will, to be in control

在宅
(zai-taku)
to be at home

土地
(to-chi)
land

地球
(chi-kyū)
the earth

地獄
(ji-goku)
hell

地方
(chi-hō)
local regions

地
(chi, ji)
earth, land

The original meaning of "to wind along" led to this character being used to represent "the earth", "land", "nation", "location", "status", "native" and "true character".

地震
(ji-shin)
earthquake

観光地
(kan-kō-chi)
tourist area

地蔵
(ji-zō)
A small statue often found on streets and in temples. It represents a god who protects the souls of travelers and children.

圧
(atsu)
pressure

The original meaning of this character was "to press against". This was derived from the process of using soil to fill in things in order to seal or block them. Its meanings now include "to press", "to crush", "to oppress" and "to control".

圧倒的
(attō-teki)
overwhelming

水圧
(sui-atsu)
water pressure

高血圧
(kō-ketsu-atsu)
hypertension
→ 低血圧
(tei-ketsu-atsu)
low blood pressure

平均
(hei-kin)
average

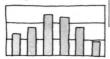

均
(kin, nara-su, hito-shi-i)
level

From the original meaning of "to level ground", this kanji took on the meaning of "to equalize", "average" and "equal".

均一
(kin-itsu)
uniform (100円均一 means that everything costs 100 yen)

堂
(dō)
hall

The essential meaning of this kanji is "a building where many people can gather". It is used for "hall", "auditorium" and such ideas as "loud voice" and "fair and honest".

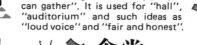

食堂
(shoku-dō)
cafeteria

礼拝堂
(rei-hai-dō)
chapel, synagogue

堂々
(dō-dō)
solemn, wise (々 indicates a repetition of the preceding character)

坂道
(saka-michi)
a road on a hill

→ 上り坂
(nobo-ri-zaka)
going uphill

← → 下り坂
(kuda-ri-zaka)
going downhill

These two characters are used for both physical motion and to indicate movement in social and career status.

坂
(han, saka)
slope

Derived from the ancient word for "diagonal", this character came to mean a "diagonal hill"; slope.

登坂車線
(to-han-sha-sen)
climbing lane for slow traffic

入場
(nyū-jō)
admission

← → 退場
(tai-jō)
exit

場
(jō, ba)
place

Originally used for places devoted to worshipping god, this character now means "place", "situation", "period", "a pause" and "theatrical scene".

場合
(ba-ai)
situation

市場
(ichi-ba)
wholesale market
(shi-jō)
the market,
an exchange

工場
(kō-jō)
factory

基本
(ki-hon)
essential

first...

基
(ki, motoi, moto-zuku)
basis

The original meaning of "to begin" has been expanded to include "basic", "foundation", "root" and "origin".

基地
(ki-chi)
military base

垂
(sui, ta-reru)
to hang

Modeled after the image of flowers and leaves hanging in the air, this kanji means "to hang".

垂直
(sui-choku)
to hang straight down at a 90° angle to the ground

胃下垂
(i-ka-sui)
gastroptosis

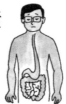

模型
(mo-kei)
model

型
(kei, kata)
model

刑 means "law". Add 土 to this and it means "earth to which rules can be applied"; a mold. This character means "model", "type" and "design". It is also used for certain set movements in jūdō and acting.

城
(jō, shiro)
castle

Devised to express the idea of "to defend", this character was later used for the building designed to protect land and people; a castle.

大阪城
(ō-saka-jō)
Osaka Castle

城下町
(jō-ka-machi)
a feudal town

堅実
(ken-jitsu)
sound, reliable

堅
(ken, kata-i)
hard

Originally used to express "hardened soil", this character is now used for all "hard" objects.

126

報道
(hō-dō)
the press

報
(hō, hō-jiru, muku-iru)
news

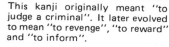

This kanji originally meant ''to judge a criminal''. It later evolved to mean ''to revenge'', ''to reward'' and ''to inform''.

情報
(jō-hō)
information

報酬
(hō-shū)
payment

増
(zō, ma-su, fu-eru)
to increase

This character is used in a wide range of meanings that are all related to ''increase''; ''wide'', ''to multiply'', ''to pile up'' and ''to spread''. It's antonym is 減 *(gen, hé-ru)* ''to decrease''.

倍増
(bai-zō)
to double

壁画
(heki-ga)
wall painting

壁
(heki, kabé)
wall

Used for a broad range of structures, this character basically means ''wall''.

壁紙
(kabé-gami)
wallpaper

学習塾
(gaku-shū-juku)
cram school

塾
(juku)
cram school

Due to the severity of competition to enter better universities in Japan, most children attend cram schools after school.

chō, tori

This pictographic character was modeled after the image of a bird.

Meaning bird, bird species (especially for birds with long feathers)

This character appears in compounds that are related to birds.

渡り鳥

(wata-ri-dori)
migrational bird

渡 means to cross a body of water. Combined with 鳥 it indicates birds that migrate with the changing seasons.

鳥瞰図

(chō-kan-zu)
overhead map

瞰 means to look down. This compound means a map drawn from a bird's-eye view.

白鳥

(haku-chō)
swan

白 means white.

閑古鳥

(kan-ko-dori)
cuckoo

When someone says that "a cuckoo can be heard at that store"
閑古鳥が鳴く *(kan-ko-dori-ga-na-ku)*, it indicates a store with few customers.

鳴
(mei, na-ku, na-ru)
to chirp

This character's original design of a mouth and a rooster indicated the process of announcing the time. This was later expanded to include "bird calls", "to ring" and "to be well-known". ➡

雷鳴
(rai-mei)
thunder

悲鳴
(hi-mei)
shriek

鶴
(kaku, tsuru)
crane

鶏
(kei, niwatori)
cock

鷗
(kamomé)
sea gull

鷲
(washi)
eagle

鴨
(kamo)
duck

鷺
(sagi)
heron

雁
(gan, kari)
wild goose

鳩
(kyū, hato)
pigeon

鷹
(taka)
hawk

鶯
(uguisu)
Japanese nightingale

鴛鴦
(oshidori)
mandarin duck

gyo, sakana

This pictographic character was modeled after the image of a fish.

魚

 ⇨ ⇨ ⇨ 魚

Meaning fish

This character appears in compounds that are related to fish.

魚介類
(gyo-kai-rui)
seafood

魚雷
(gyo-rai)
torpedo

雷 means thunder (see p. 129). This therefore means something that travels through the water like a fish and has a thunderous effect; torpedo.

木魚
(moku-gyo)
wooden drum

This is a special type of drum carved from wood in the shape of a fish. It is held by Buddhist monks while they read the sutras.

人魚
(nin-gyo)
mermaid

130

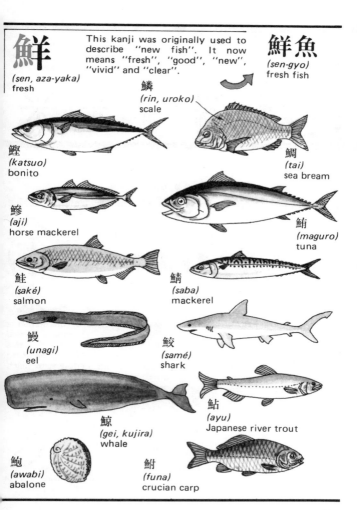

鮮
(sen, aza-yaka)
fresh

This kanji was originally used to describe "new fish". It now means "fresh", "good", "new", "vivid" and "clear".

鮮魚
(sen-gyo)
fresh fish

鱗
(rin, uroko)
scale

鰹
(katsuo)
bonito

鯛
(tai)
sea bream

鯵
(aji)
horse mackerel

鮪
(maguro)
tuna

鮭
(saké)
salmon

鯖
(saba)
mackerel

鰻
(unagi)
eel

鮫
(samé)
shark

鯨
(gei, kujira)
whale

鮎
(ayu)
Japanese river trout

鮑
(awabi)
abalone

鮒
(funa)
crucian carp

bei, mai, komé

This pictographic character was drawn from the image of a millet crest.

Meaning rice, standard of measurement equivalent to a meter, used to indicate America (see p. 65.)

This character appears in compounds that are related to rice.

米俵
(komé-dawara)
straw rice bag

A 俵 is a straw bag for carrying commodities.

米国
(bei-koku)
America

When written out in kanji, "America" is written phonetically as 亜米利加. This is abbreviated to 米国.

米寿
(bei-ju)
88th birthday celebration

米 is composed of the elements 八十八. 八 means 8 and 十 means 10. Therefore, this character can be broken down to 8 10 8, or 88. People who reach this age celebrate their good fortune.

米粒
(komé-tsubu)
a grain of rice

粒 means "grain" and is used for objects with a similar shape.

粉
(fun, kona, ko)
powder

This character was originally used for fine powder made from rice bran and used as facial cosmetics. When rice is soaked in water a layer of fine particles settles on the bottom. This is gathered and from it face powder is made. This led to the meanings of "flour", "powder" and "dust".

花粉
(ka-fun)
pollen

小麦粉
(ko-mugi-ko)
wheat flour

粉石鹸
(kona-sekken)
powdered soap

料
(ryō)
charge

This kanji was derived from the process of measuring something. It came to mean "to measure the amount of rice". It now means "to estimate", "to consider" and "charge or rate".

原料
(gen-ryō)
raw materials

食料品
(shoku-ryō-hin)
foodstuffs

入場料
(nyū-jō-ryō)
admission charge

料理
(ryō-ri)
cooking

奇数
(ki-sū)
odd number

←→ 偶数
(gū-sū)
even number

17
19
21
23
25
......

数
(sū, kazu, kazo-eru)
number

This character means "to count" and "number".

人数
(nin-zū)
the number of people

粋
(sui, iki)
purity

This character was originally used to describe the pure white powder recovered after soaking rice 粉 . This led to the meanings of "purity", "essence", "good" and later on "chic" and "stylish".

純粋
(jun-sui)
pure

粋人
(sui-jin)
a refined man

精
(sei, shō, shira-geru)
spirit

Based on the idea of "cleanliness", this character described rice that had been selected for its cleanliness. This led to the following meanings: "white", "detailed", "pure", "spirit", "correct" and "to do detailed work".

精神
(sei-shin)
mind, spirit

妖精
(yō-sei)
fairy

精算所
(sei-san-jo)
passenger fare-adjustment office

精密
(sei-mitsu)
precision

砂糖
(sa-tō)
sugar

糖
(tō)
sugar

This character was first used to mean "rice barley". This barley was used to make sweet candies. From here it took on the meaning of "sweet".

Foods Made With Rice

ご飯
(go-han)
boiled rice

wash the rice

electric rice cooker

餅
(mochi)
rice cakes

cook the *mochi-gomé* (glutinous rice)

pound the rice

mold it into small egg shapes

煎餅
(sen-bei)
rice cracker

cut the pounded rice

dip it into soy sauce and bake it again

まんじゅう
(man-jū)
steamed bun

knead wheat flour

wrap the sweetened bean paste with kneaded flour

steam it

団子
(dan-go)
rice dumpling

rice flour

steam it

mold it into small ball shapes

酒
(saké)
rice wine

steamed rice

malted rice

ferment the mix

squeeze

mon, kado

門

This character was drawn from the image of two closed doors.

口口 ⇒ 閂 ⇒ 門 ⇒ 門

Meaning gate, entrance, the beginning of things, house, lineage, classification, alumni

This character is used in compounds that are related to gates.

門限
(mon-gen)
curfew

限 means "limit". At night gates are shut to keep out unwanted visitors. Curfews are quite common in dormitories and for children living at home.

入門
(nyū-mon)
entrance

The "entrance" here is an abstract one. It is an entrance to a new world, a new academic field or unknown terrain. A 入門書 is a guide-book for beginners.

専門
(sen-mon)
specialty

専 means "to concentrate one's energy into one area". A person who is well-versed in a particular area is called a 専門家 *(sen-mon-ka)*.

門前払い
(mon-zen-bara-i)
to turn away

The combination of 門, 前 (see p. 38) and 払 (to pay) creates the notion of "to pay before entering". This naturally includes turning away those who cannot pay: "to turn away" and "to refuse to see".

閉
(hei, to-jiru, shi-meru)
to close

才 is drawn in the shape of a wooden barrier used to close a gate. Combined with 門 it means "to shut", "to hide", "to stop", "to end" and "to block".

閉店
(hei-ten)
a store's closing time

← → 開店
(kai-ten)
opening time

閉会
(hei-kai)
to adjourn a meeting

← → 開会
(kai-kai)
to open a meeting

密閉
(mippei)
tightly closed

開放
(kai-hō)
liberation

開
(kai, hira-ku)
to open

Derived from the idea of "to break away from", this character means "to open", "to spread out", "to confide" and "to begin".

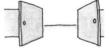

開花
(kai-ka)
to bloom

開発
(kai-hatsu)
to develop

開演
(kai-en)
curtain time

開運
(kai-un)
luck, fortune

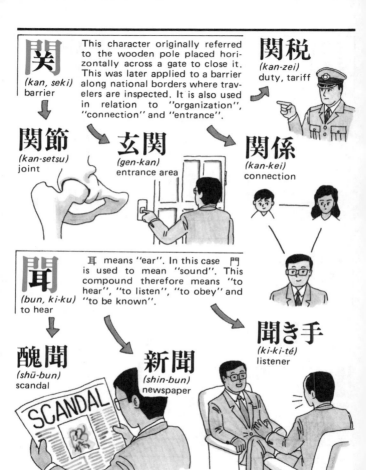

関
(kan, seki)
barrier

This character originally referred to the wooden pole placed horizontally across a gate to close it. This was later applied to a barrier along national borders where travelers are inspected. It is also used in relation to "organization", "connection" and "entrance".

関税
(kan-zei)
duty, tariff

関節
(kan-setsu)
joint

玄関
(gen-kan)
entrance area

関係
(kan-kei)
connection

聞
(bun, ki-ku)
to hear

耳 means "ear". In this case 門 is used to mean "sound". This compound therefore means "to hear", "to listen", "to obey" and "to be known".

醜聞
(shū-bun)
scandal

SCANDAL

新聞
(shin-bun)
newspaper

聞き手
(ki-ki-té)
listener

間
(kan, ken, aida, ma)
space

The origin of this character can be traced to spaces between the doors of a gate. It took on the meanings "space between things", "period of time", "free time", "place", "recently", "reasonable", "sometimes", "room" and "secretly".

間接
(kan-setsu)
indirect

← → 直接
(choku-setsu)
direct

時間
(ji-kan)
time, hour

間一髪
(kan-ippatsu)
a close call,
a hair's breadth

Japanese Houses

間 is used as a suffix in the names of most Japanese rooms.

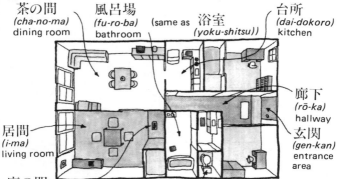

茶の間
(cha-no-ma)
dining room

風呂場
(fu-ro-ba)
bathroom

(same as 浴室 *(yoku-shitsu)*)

台所
(dai-dokoro)
kitchen

居間
(i-ma)
living room

床の間
(toko-no-ma)

廊下
(rō-ka)
hallway

玄関
(gen-kan)
entrance area

便所
(ben-jo) toilet (this word has almost entirely been replaced by トイレ *(to-i-ré)*; a direct translation of the English word.)

In traditional rooms with straw *tatami* mats there is often a small space where the floor is raised slightly. Flowers and decorative drawings are displayed here.

bai, kai

貝

This character was modeled after the image of a cowrie shell.

Meaning shellfish, shell, a beautiful brocade, valuables (in the past sea shells were used as money.)

二枚貝
(ni-mai-gai)
clam

→ 巻き貝
(ma-ki-gai)
snail, conch

This term is used to refer to a variety of sea creatures with a 2-valved shell.

貝柱
(kai-bashira)
shell ligament

This is the muscular tissue that clams use to open and close their shells. This part of scallops and certain other clams is eaten.

貝合わせ
(kai-a-wa-sé)
an ancient game

Clam shells were decorated with drawings and poems and then the two halves separated and mixed with others. The object of the game was to find two shells that formed a pair.

貝塚
(kai-zuka)
shell mound

There have been many discoveries of ancient mounds that contain shells and earthen and stone implements that were used by primitive man during the Stone Age.

負
(fu, ma-keru, o-u)
to lose

The combination of a person and 貝 meant "to be in debt". Modern meanings include "to depend on", "to ask", "to lose", "to disobey" and "responsibility". This kanji is also used with negative numbers.

勝負
(shō-bu)
a sports match

負傷
(fu-shō)
injury

財産
(zai-san)
estate

財
(zai)
wealth

This character's original meaning of "to pile up" was used to refer to "stored cargo". This led to the meanings of "valuables" and "value".

財布
(sai-fu)
wallet

文化財
(bun-ka-zai)
cultural assets

貨幣
(ka-hei)
currency

貨
(ka)
freight

When used alone, the top portion of this character 化 means "to change". Combined with 貝 (money), this means "something that is exchanged for money"; "cargo".

百貨店
(hyakka-ten)
department store

雑貨
(zakka)
general merchandise

141

費
(hi, tsui-yasu)
expense

Based on the idea of "to get rid of", this kanji refers to the process of spending money. Its meanings include "to spend", "to diminish", "to waste time" and "costs".

経費
(kei-hi)
business expenses

浪費
(rō-hi)
waste, extravagance

資源
(shi-gen)
resources

資
(shi)
capital

This character originally meant "to stockpile money". It now means "commodities", "funds", "to assist", "merit", "resource", and "costs".

投資
(tō-shi)
to invest

資料
(shi-ryō)
data

資格
(shi-kaku)
qualification

賃
(chin)
hire

From the original meaning of "to do work", this character came to mean "payment for work performed".

運賃
(un-chin)
passenger fare, freight charges

家賃
(ya-chin)
rent

月

物質
(busshitsu)
matter

質
(shitsu, shichi)
quality

This character was originally used to mean "money" 金. It later gained its present meanings of "the essence", "ingredient", "pure" and "to ask relentlessly".

人質
(hito-jichi)
hostage

質屋
(shichi-ya)
pawn shop

質問
(shitsu-mon)
question

賞金
(shō-kin)
prize money

賞
(shō, ho-meru)
to praise

This kanji was originally used to describe "an award given by a high ranking person to someone of a lower status." This came to mean "praise". It also means "to fully enjoy beauty and goodness".

賞味
(shō-mi)
to relish

ノーベル賞
(nō-bé-ru-shō)
Nobel prize

鑑賞
(kan-shō)
to appreciate

143

売
(bai, u-ru)
to sell

The combination of 出 "to put out" and 買 clearly means "to put something out for sale", "to market" and "to do business".

売店
(bai-ten)
a sales stand

新発売
(shin-hatsu-bai)
newly released product

NEW

買収
(bai-shū)
to buy out

買
(bai, ka-u)
to purchase

This originally was used to mean "to barter". It now means "to purchase", "to fix a price", "to invite trouble" and "to receive".

買い物
(ka-i-mono)
to shop

責任
(seki-nin)
responsibility

責
(seki, se-meru)
to condemn

Originally used to indicate shells used for billing purposes, this kanji now means "to blame", "to censure" and "duty towards others".

通信販売
(tsū-shin-han-bai)
mail-order sales

販
(han)
trade

The combination of 貝 and an element that means to return 反 represents "to exchange something for money"; "to trade".

SHOPPING
1 2 ²

貧乏
(bin-bō)
poverty

MONEY!

貧
(hin, bin,
mazu-shi-i)
poor

The basic meaning of this character is "financially poor". However, it is also used to indicate "poor" in such areas as "ability and conditions" and "few in number".

貧弱
(hin-jaku)
feeble

貧血
(hin-ketsu)
anemia

貴
(ki, tatto-i)
noble

The original meaning of "many" referred in particular to "many" 貝 . "Esteemed", "valuable" and "honored" are all expressed with this character.

貴族
(ki-zoku)
aristocracy

貴重品
(ki-chō-hin)
valuable object

貴金属
(ki-kin-zoku)
precious metals

貯金
(cho-kin)
savings

貯金通帳

貯
(cho, takuwa-eru)
to store

The basic idea of this character is "to collect in large amounts"; to stockpile.

賃貸
(chin-tai)
to lease

FOR RENT

貸
(tai, ka-su)
to lend

From the original idea of "to make a payment easy" this character came to mean "to lease", "to help" and "generosity".

This character was modeled after the image of a flame.

Meaning fire, to burn

This kanji is used in compounds that are related to fire or burning.

火事
(ka-ji)
a fire

花火
(hana-bi)
fireworks

Since 花 means flower, this compound literally means "fire flowers". Fireworks are an important part of summer festivals throughout Japan.

火気厳禁
(ka-ki-gen-kin)
Fires Prohibited

This compound can be seen displayed in places like gasoline stations where there is a strong danger of a fire spreading.

漁火
(isari-bi)
fisherman's fire lure

漁 means "to fish". At night fishermen use fires and lights to attract fish.

灰
(kai, hai)
ash

The original meaning of this character was "to become black". It later was used to indicate the blackened remains of a burnt object; ash. It also means "something that has lost its vitality".

灰色
(hai-iro)
gray

火山灰
(ka-zan-bai)
volcanic ash

火山
(ka-zan)
means "volcano"

街灯
(gai-tō)
streetlamp

灯
(tei, chō, tō, akari, tomoshibi)
lamp

This character is used for many sources of illumination.

点灯
(ten-tō)
to turn on a light

炎
(en, honoo)
flame

This combination of two 火 refers to the heart of a fire; the flame. It is used to mean "to burn", "flame", "violence", "severity", "heat" and "to burn brightly".

炎症
(en-shō)
inflammation

炎上
(en-jō)
destruction of a large building by fire

炎天下
(en-ten-ka)
under the scorching sun

147

災
(sai, wazawa-i)
disaster

This originally referred to disasters that result from fire, but it is now used for all man-made and natural calamities.

天災
(ten-sai)
natural disaster such as an earthquake

防災
(bō-sai)
disaster prevention

自然
(shi-zen)
natural

然
(zen, nen)
in that way

Although this character originally meant "to burn", it later took on the meaning of "in a certain way". It is now used for "in a set way", "however", "nevertheless" and "if so".

偶然
(gū-zen)
coincidental

燃料
(nen-ryō)
fuel

燃
(nen, mo-eru)
to burn

By adding a 火 to 然, that character's original meaning of "to burn" was reinforced.

不燃性
(fu-nen-sei)
nonflammable

煙
(en, kemuri)
smoke

The original meaning of this word was "to hang over" in the way mist hangs over a village in the morning. This led to "smoke", "to fume", "to regret" and "tobacco".

煙草
(tabako)
This combination of 煙 and 草 "grass" was created to mean "tobacco".

NO SMOKING

禁煙
(kin-en)
no smoking

148

焼き餅

(ya-ki-mochi)
grilled rice cake,
jealousy

←

焼
(shō, ya-ku)
to burn, to grill

This character is used to mean "to
burn food"; grilling, roasting, and
baking. It also means "to take
care" and "to envy".

焼香
(shō-kō)
incense offering

お好み焼き
(o-kono-mi-ya-ki)
a grilled pancake with
meat, seafood and
vegetables.

熟
(juku)
ripe

This character was first used to
mean "to soften" and "to boil".
It later evolved to mean "to ripen",
"to mature", and "to master".

熟睡
(juku-sui)
sound sleep

熟漢
語字

未熟
(mi-juku)
unripe, premature

熟語
(juku-go)
compounds construct-
ed from two or more
kanji

熱湯
(nettō)
boiling water

←

熱
(netsu, atsu-i)
heat

This character first described the
heat of a fire. Later it came to
mean "heat", "feverishness" and
"passion".

熱中
(netchū)
zeal

熱帯
(nettai)
the tropics

149

u, amé

雨

This character is a drawing of water falling from the sky.

Meaning rain

This kanji is used in compounds related to rain and clouds.

雨雲
(ama-gumo)
rain clouds

雨量
(u-ryō)
rainfall

暴風雨
(bō-fū-u)
storm

梅雨
(tsuyu, bai-u)
rainy season

暴 means "violent" and 風 means "wind". This three-character compound therefore means "violent wind and rain"; storm.

Every year during June and July there is a period of approximately one month during which rain falls almost everyday in Japan.

電
(den)
electricity

This character is drawn from a combination of lightning and a rain drop. It means "lightning", "electricity" and "very fast".

電車
(den-sha)
train

電光石火
(den-kō-sekka)
This combination of a lightning flash 電光 and a spark 石火 means "extremely fast".

電気
(den-ki)
electricity

電信柱
(den-shin-bashira)
telephone pole
(abbreviated to 電柱 *den-chū*).

停電
(tei-den)
blackout

電話
(den-wa)
telephone

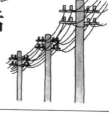

露草
(tsuyu-kusa)
a day flower

露
(ro, tsuyu)
dew

Based on the image of a series of grains, this character is used to describe the phenomenon of humidity becoming like grains; dew. It also means "wet", "to expose", "bare", "to become thin" and "to be few in number".

暴露
(baku-ro)
to expose

披露宴
(hi-rō-en)
a reception party

雪
(setsu, yuki)
snow

From the idea of "pure beauty", this character came to mean "snow". Its other meanings include "to purify", "to erase" and "white".

雪辱
(setsu-joku)
to avenge

初雪
(hatsu-yuki)
first snowfall of the year

雲海
(un-kai)
a sea of clouds

雲
(un, kumo)
cloud

The inspiration for this character was the image of swirling clouds. In addition to "cloud", it is used for "high objects" and "fluffy objects".

雲泥の差
(un-dei-no-sa)
a wide difference

The combination of a cloud and 泥 "mud" indicates the total contrast between "high and lofty" and "low and soiled".

需
(ju)
request

The original meaning of this character was "to get wet (from the rain)". It now means "to seek", "to demand" and "something that is necessary".

必需品
(hitsu-ju-hin)
a necessity

亡霊
(bō-rei)
a departed soul

霊長類
(rei-chō-rui)
a leader with miraculous powers; mankind

霊
(rei)
soul

The original design of this character included 雨 and many mouths. It represents "the spirit of the dead", "supernatural" and "holy".

152

飛行機雲
(hi-kō-ki-gumo)
jet stream,
condensation trail

入道雲
(nyū-dō-gumo)
gigantic columns of
clouds; cumulonimbus

いわし雲
(i-wa-shi-gumo)
a small, white, fleecy
cloud; cirrocumulus

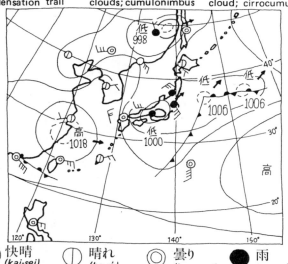

○ 快晴
(kai-sei)
fair and clear

◑ 晴れ
(ha-ré)
clear

◎ 曇り
(kumo-ri)
cloudy

● 雨
(u, amé)
rain

◒ 雷
(rai, kaminari)
thunder, thunderbolt

◉ 霧
(mu, kiri)
fog

⊢ 風向風力
(fū-kō-fū-ryoku)
wind derection and speed

*shoku, jiki,
tabé-ru, ku-u*

食

This character was formed by the combination of the image of food piled high in a cooking utensil and ⌄ , which has phonetic value.

Meaning food, to eat, to live, to chew

This character is used in compounds that are related to food or eating and drinking.

食欲
(shoku-yoku)
appetite

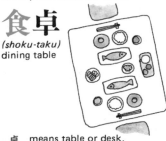

Since 欲 means desire, this is obviously the desire for food.

非常食
(hi-jō-shoku)
emergency rations

Food prepared and stored in case of earthquakes or other disasters.

食卓
(shoku-taku)
dining table

卓 means table or desk.

月食
(gesshoku)
lunar eclipse
(the moon is "eaten" by the earth's shadow).

→日食
(nisshoku)
solar eclipse

飲
(in, no-mu)
to drink

The original form of this character showed a person with his mouth wide open about to drink *saké*. It means "to drink", "a drink", "revelry" and "to tolerate".

清涼飲料水
(sei-ryō-in-ryō-sui)
soft drinks

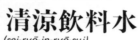

炊飯器
(sui-han-ki)
rice cooker

飯
(han, meshi)
food

This character was derived from the idea of "to place in the mouth". It means "to eat", "a meal" and "edible rice and grains".

栄養
(ei-yō)
nutrition

養
(yō, yashina-u)
to raise

This character was derived from the idea "to prepare food". It later came to mean "to feed", "to raise", "to educate" and "nutritional food".

装飾
(sō-shoku)
decoration

飾
(shoku, kaza-ru)
to decorate

The 食 in this character only has phonetic value. Beginning with the idea of "to wipe", this kanji came to mean "to wipe clean", "to decorate", "to adorn" and "to beautify".

博物館
(haku-butsu-kan)
museum

館
(kan, yakata)
hall

The origin of this character can be traced to the idea of "house". It first was used as "a dining room for visitors". It now means "mansion", "inn" and other large buildings.

EATING OUT
日本語のメニュー

Menus in restaurants are usually written in Japanese only. It is convenient to learn the names of a few common dishes to facilitate ordering.

蕎麦屋 *(so-ba-ya)* noodle shop

Soba is a brown noodle made of buckwheat. It is one of the staple products of the traditional Japanese diet. *Soba* is served in many forms but perhaps the most common is as a thick soup with vegetables, meat and fish. うどん *(u-do-n)* is another kind of noodle that can be eaten at a *sobaya*. It is whitish, made from wheat flour and thicker than *soba*. Rice dishes are also available at a *sobaya*.

きそば
(ki-so-ba)
Plain *soba* with nothing mixed in the soup.

天ぷらそば
(ten-pu-ra-so-ba)
Tempura is vegetables and fish that have been deep fried in a thick batter. It is often mixed with *soba* in one dish.

五目そば
(go-moku-so-ba)
soba mixed with many vegetables and meat.

天丼
(ten-don)
丼 means "bowl". There are many 丼 dishes made from a bowl of rice with something on top. 天丼 comes with *tempura*.

親子丼
(oya-ko-don)
親 means parent and 子 means child. This dish is made with diced chicken and eggs, therefore 親子丼.

かつ重
(ka-tsu-jū)
かつ *(ka-tsu)* is an example of *gairaigo* (see p. 13). A かつ is a deep fried pork cutlet. かつ重 is a pork cutlet on a bed of rice in a square lunch box.

156

寿司屋
(su-shi-ya)
Sushi shop

にぎり
(ni-gi-ri)
Raw fish and other things are placed on a bite-size ball of rice.

ちらし
(chi-ra-shi)
Fish and other things are placed on a bed of rice in a container.

のり巻
(no-ri-maki)
Kampyō (dried gourd shavings) surrounded by rice and wrapped in the shape of a cone or cylinder with a covering of dried seaweed.

松	*(shō, matsu)* superior	特上	*(toku-jō)* excellent
竹	*(chiku, také)* excellent	上	*(jō)* good
梅	*(bai, umé)* good	並	*(nami)* normal

Rankings

Certain characters are used to rank foods, menus, inn rooms and other things related to luxury.

納豆巻
(nattō-maki)
a のり巻 made with a paste of fermented soy beans

鉄火巻
(tekka-maki)
a のり巻 made with raw tuna

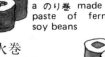

喫茶店
(kissa-ten)
Coffee Shops

Large and small 喫茶店 can be found almost everywhere. In the past they served tea but now they serve an assortment of drinks, snacks and cakes. These are good places to go and kill time while reading a book.

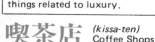

コーヒー
(kō-hī)
coffee

アイス コーヒー
(a-i-su-kō-hī)
iced coffee

紅茶
(kō-cha)
black tea

オレンジ ジュース
(o-ré-n-ji-jū-su)
orange juice

クリーム ソーダ
(ku-ri-mu-sō-da)
cream soda

サンドイッチ
(sa-n-do-itchi)
sandwich (eggsalad, tuna and cheese are common.)

モーニング
(mō-ni-n-gu)
breakfast set of toast and coffee

スパゲッティ
(su-pa-getti)
spaghetti

ランチセット
(ra-n-chi-setto)
lunch set

SIGNS AND DISPLAYS AROUND TOWN
街頭でみかける標識、標示

禁　煙　*(kin-en)*
No Smoking

(migi-gawa-tsū-kō)
Keep to the Right

左側通行
(hidari-gawa-tsū-kō)
Keep to the Left

(chi-ka-tetsu)
Subway

(mi-do-ri-no-mado-guchi)
Green (First Class and Long Distance Ticket) Window

大　人　*(otona)*
adult

小　人　*(kodomo)*
child

故　障　*(ko-shō)*
Out of Order

(hi-jō-guchi)
Emergency Exit

入　口　*(iri-guchi)*
Entrance

出　口　*(dē-guchi)*
Exit

危　険　*(ki-ken)*
Danger!

(ta-ku-shī-no-ri-ba)
Taxi Stand

満　車　*(man-sha)*
Full

駐車場　*(chū-sha-jō)*
Parking Lot

空　車　*(kū-sha)*
Space Available

KANJI
CULTURE
漢字の文化

KANJI AND THE CALENDAR
漢字と暦

The ancient Chinese used 10 characters to name the ten months of their calendar and 12 characters for the 12 constellations of the Zodiac. Soothsayers used combinations of these characters to predict the future. Before the adoption of the Western calendar the Japanese too used the lunar calendar and performed similar rites.

十干 *(jikkan)* **the ten calendar signs**

甲 *(kō)*	乙 *(otsu)*	丙 *(hei)*	丁 *(tei)*	戊 *(bo)*
己 *(ki)*	庚 *(kō)*	辛 *(shin)*	壬 *(jin)*	癸 *(ki)*

十二支 *(jū-ni-shi)* **the twelve signs of the zodiac**

子
(né) the Rat   丑 *(ushi)* the Ox   寅 *(tora)* the Tiger   卯 *(u)* the Rabbit

辰
(tatsu) the Dragon   巳 *(mi)* the Snake   午 *(uma)* the Horse   未 *(hitsuji)* the Sheep

申
(saru) the Monkey   酉 *(tori)* the Cock   戌 *(inu)* the Dog   亥 *(i)* the Boar

六曜 *(roku-yō)*

The lunar calendar consists of units of six days. Each day has a name which expresses its peculiar qualities as defined according to ancient soothsaying techniques. This system is no longer used as a calendar in Japan, but the mystical implications of the particular days are still considered of importance when official ceremonies such as weddings and funerals are held.

先勝
(sen-gachi, sen-shō)
This is a good day for important events as long as they are held in the morning. It is not advisable to hold an event in the afternoon on this day.

仏滅
(butsu-metsu)
A bad day for beginning things. Marriages, store openings and anything related to "beginning" should be avoided.

友引
(tomo-biki)
友 means "friend" and 引 means "to pull". Funerals are not held on this day because of the fear that the deceased will "pull a friend along" out of this world.

大安
(tai-an)
Things done on this day are blessed with fortune. The best day for weddings.

先負
(sen-maké, sen-bu)
Discretion is the key word on this day. One should be careful with important affairs and avoid serious decisions.

赤口
(shakkō, shakku)
A bad day all around. Important events should be avoided.

TANKA AND HAIKU
短歌と俳句

Tanka are traditional Japanese poems that conform to a set composition. A *tanka* has 5 lines that have 5, 7, 5, 7 and 7 syllables respectively, for a total of 31 syllables. *Tanka* first appeared towards the end of the 8th century during the latter part of the Nara Period.

The oldest remaining collection of written Japanese literature is the *Man'yōshū* 万葉集 . It contains poems and prose written over approximately 400 years, including pieces written by Emperor *Nintoku* who reigned from the year 313 until 399 and works written until the reign of Emperor *Junnin* (758-764). All of the collection is written in *man'yōgana* 万葉仮名 .

The *tanka* written during this period are imbued with a stern realism and a vital force.

Tanka were used in many traditional card games and have maintained great popularity since ancient times.

During the *Heian* Period, (794 - 1185), the aristocratic class was firmly in power. They preferred a more idealistic style that placed great emphasis on technique. During this period *hiragana* was devised and *tanka* came to be written with these new characters in a free-flowing style.

Haiku are shorter than *tanka*. They consist of three lines of 5, 7 and 5 syllables respectively. *Haiku* are fundamentally related to nature and always include words that bring forth images of natural phenomena. Among the masterpieces of this genre are beautifully terse expressions of the beauty of nature and the tragedy of human sufferings.

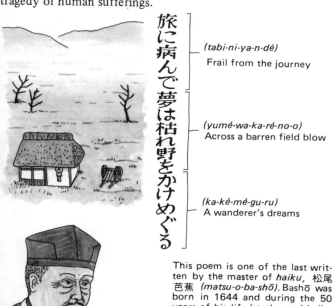

旅に病んで夢は枯れ野をかけめぐる

(tabi-ni-ya-n-dé)
Frail from the journey

(yumé-wa-ka-ré-no-o)
Across a barren field blow

(ka-ké-mé-gu-ru)
A wanderer's dreams

This poem is one of the last written by the master of *haiku*, 松尾 芭蕉 *(matsu-o-ba-shō)*. Bashō was born in 1644 and during the 50 years of his life he elevated *haiku* from a mere pastime to an art in which the richness of the Japanese language is seen in pure form. Bashō spent most of his life wandering throughout the land and left behind a legacy that has endeared him to the hearts of the Japanese of every generation since.

163

CARD GAMES WITH CHARACTERS
文字のカードゲーム

Played during the New Year's Holidays, かるた *(ka-ru-ta)* is a favorite among traditional card games. In order to explain the rules for this game it is first necessary to introduce the types of cards that are used.

百人一首
(hyaku-nin-isshu)
The 100 Tanka by the 100 Celebrated Poets

Based on a collection of 100 *tanka*, this set of 200 cards consists of 100 pairs, each of which has the five lines of a *tanka* written on one card and the final two lines on another. There is a drawing of the author of the *tanka* on the upper card.

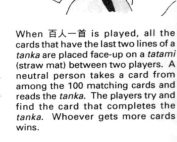

When 百人一首 is played, all the cards that have the last two lines of a *tanka* are placed face-up on a *tatami* (straw mat) between two players. A neutral person takes a card from among the 100 matching cards and reads the *tanka*. The players try and find the card that completes the *tanka*. Whoever gets more cards wins.

いろはがるた
(i-ro-ha-ga-ru-ta)
Iroha Cards

いろは is the beginning of the traditional ordering system for the 48 basic *hiragana*. Each card has a proverb that begins with one of the *hiragana* characters. In addition, there are 48 cards with drawings that express the moral of the proverb.

When played with いろは cards, the card with a picture is placed on the *tatami* mat and the proverb is read. The object is the same.

偏旁かるた
(hen-tsukuri-ka-ru-ta)

Kanji element cards

A 偏 *(hen)* is an abbreviated form of a pictographic kanji that is used as the left side of compound ideographs. In this book we have introduced several 偏 including the *sanzui* 氵, *tehen* 扌 and *ninben* 亻. 旁 *(tsu-ku-ri)* are the elements that appear on the right side of compound charac-

ters. This set of cards has approximately 50 cards with different 偏 and about 100 cards with 旁. The object of the game is to arrange the cards to form compound characters. This game was very popular in the 1700s during the *Edo* Period (1600 - 1867) but is no longer played.

KANJI AND THE OCCULT
オカルトとしての漢字

Kanji have been used in many areas and by many cultures over the past 3000 years. In many cases we can see ways in which kanji have been influenced and changed by local folkways and cultural peculiarities. We find a common conception that kanji are not simply written characters that express an idea, but symbols containing mysterious powers. The notion of kanji playing a mysterious role is still very much alive in modern Japanese culture.

Pothooks Formed in the Shape of 水

In the past, Japanese houses were built with a hearth in the center of the main room which warmed the house and was used for cooking. Hanging above the fire was a device that could be used to control the position of a pot over the fire. In order to increase its resistance to fire and prevent the fire from spreading, these pothooks were made in the shape of the character for water 水.

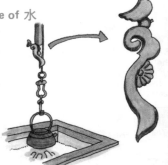

Offers of Thanks and Charms

Influences of the Buddhist precepts that were transmitted to Japan can be found firmly rooted in ancient legends and *Shintō* 神道 beliefs. One of these is the notion that small charms with characters written on them have the power to ward off evil spirits.

お守り
(o-mamo-ri)
Charms
A piece of paper or wood with an incantation is wrapped in a small cloth. If kept close to the body at all times, such charms are thought to keep misfortune away and bring good luck.

Charms from the Suitengū Shrine to Ensure Safe Delivery

The Suitengū Shrine in Tokyo is famous for the many women who visit there to pray for a safe pregnancy and easy delivery. This shrine's charm has a piece of paper with five kanji written on it. If the kanji are torn off and swallowed in the correct order a woman is guaranteed an easy delivery.

火災除け *(ka-sai-yo-ké)* a talisman to prevent fires

八方除け *(happō-yo-ké)* a talisman to ward off disaster from eight directions

盗難除け *(tō-nan-yo-ké)* a talisman to prevent theft

御札 are hung at the entrance to houses to protect the family that lives there.

御札
(o-fuda)
Talisman

These are long scrolls with sutras, incantations and the names of temples written on them to protect their bearers. Special ceremonies are performed before they are given to someone in order to imbue the talisman with its power.

Burning Letters

During the middle of August (July in some parts) the Buddhist Festival of the Departed Souls お盆 *(o-bon)* is held throughout Japan. At this time a family welcomes home the souls of its ancestors. At the end of the festival, when the souls are to depart back to their world, large fires in the shape of the character 大 "large" are lit on mountain sides throughout Japan to help guide the ancestors back to their world.

The Bonfires of Kyoto

Kyoto is well-known for the immense fires lit at this time on the five mountains that surround the city. In addition to 大 , 妙 "profound reason", 法 "buddhist precepts" and other kanji, the designs of a ship and a *Shintō* gate are drawn by the blazing flames.

The Story of Earless Hōichi

Once upon a time a blind lute player named Hōichi 芳一 lived in a small seashore village called Dan-no-ura 壇の浦 . Long before, this village had been the home to the Heiké Clan 平家 , a fierce *samurai* family. However, the entire Heiké Clan was killed in a great battle. It was said that the restless souls of the dead warriors still wandered the area at night.

One night Hōichi was visited by a Heiké *samurai*. This stranger said that he had heard of Hōichi's talent and that he longed to hear him play. Blind as he was, Hōichi did not know that his visitor was a ghost and allowed himself to be led by the hand to the spot where the visitor asked him to play. All night long Hōichi charmed the spirit with his lute.

The next night Hōichi was again visited by this stranger. Again he allowed himself to be led out of his home so he could play for this man. Again he charmed him with his songs. This happened again on the third night. However, by now the chief priest of the temple where Hōichi lived had begun to suspect something.

He had one of the monks follow Hōichi. When the monk brought Hōichi back he explained how he had walked to the grave mound of the Heiké Clan and played his lute for the departed spirits.

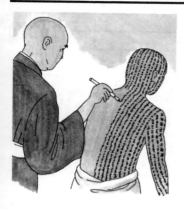

The chief priest knew that he had to protect Hōichi from the Heiké ghost. On his entire body he wrote incantations from the holy sutras, thus rendering Hōichi invisible to the wandering spirit. Hōichi listened as the priest told him "Tonight when the spirit comes to call you mustn't reply. You mustn't move an inch. This is a vital moment for you. If you are to escape this demon you must sit quietly and wait for it to leave. Do not worry, the power of the sutras will protect you."

That evening the spirit returned in search of Hōichi. The blindman did exactly as he had been told. The sutras were written so thoroughly across his body that they made him invisible to the spirit. All this wanderer of a dead *samurai* could see was a pair of ears.

You see, in his haste, the priest had forgotten to write sutras on Hōichi's ears. The spirit grabbed these ears and tore them off. Hōichi was freed from the spell that the ghost had cast upon him, but his ears were gone. From then on he became known as "Earless Hōichi".

漢和辞典
(kan-wa-ji-ten)
Kanji Dictionary

A dictionary giving the meaning of combinations of kanji and words that were transmitted to Japan from China during ancient times. Especially useful for looking up the meaning of unknown kanji.

Characters in a 漢和辞典 are classified according to the element that is most influential in their composition. Kanji that use the same element are subdivided according to the number of strokes needed to write them.

When faced with an unknown kanji you should pick the element that is most central to the composition, count the total number of strokes and check under the subdivision for that stroke number in the section for that element. If you know the character's pronunciation it is easier to look it up in the index which follows the *hiragana* order.

国語辞典
(koku-go-ji-ten)
Japanese Dictionary

Useful for looking up unknown words, symbols and expressions.

Entries in Japanese dictionaries are arranged according to the 50 *hiragana* symbols. Words are first spelled out in *hiragana,* then the appropriate kanji is given and the meaning follows. Some dictionaries give examples of use as well as synonyms.

類語辞典
(rui-go-ji-ten)
Thesaurus

This kind of dictionary lists words along with their synonyms and gives an explanation of the differences in nuance.

ことわざ事典
(ko-to-wa-za-ji-ten)
Dictionary of Proverbs

The Japanese language is rich in proverbs and anecdotes that have been handed down over many centuries. This kind of dictionary explains the origin, meaning and use of proverbs.

古語辞典
(ko-go-ji-ten)
Dictionary of Archaic Words

The Japanese language has undergone many changes over the centuries. New words have entered, old ones have changed and many have disappeared. This kind of dictionary is useful when reading old manuscripts and source material.

辞典と事典

辞典 *(ji-ten)* vs. 事典 *(ji-ten)*

A 辞典 is a dictionary. It lists words in a set order and gives their explanation, pronunciation and use. Other words for dictionaries are 辞書 *(ji-sho)* and 字典 *(ji-ten)*. On the other hand, a 事典 is an encyclopedia. It lists the names of people and things in a set order and gives information concerning them.

ABBREVIATIONS
略字と略語

The kanji that appear in this book are written in their correct form as they appear in printed matter. Many of the kanji that are used today were changed after the second world war. In addition, when people write kanji they often abbreviate them to generally accepted forms to facilitate the writing process.

Here are some examples of changed and abbreviated characters:

点 *(ten)*

喜 *(ki, yoroko-bu)*

卒 *(sotsu)*

門 *(mon, kado)*

器 *(ki, utsuwa)*

職 *(shoku)*

開 *(kai, hira-ku)*

国 *(koku, kuni)*

歴 *(reki)*

閉 *(hei, shi-maru)*

歳 *(sai, toshi)*

第 *(dai)*

Common *Jukugo* compounds that contain four or more kanji are often abbreviated to 2 characters by using the first and the third kanji.

入学試験 → 入試
(nyū-gaku-shi-ken) *(nyū-shi)*
school entrance examination

免許停止 → 免停
(men-kyo-tei-shi) *(men-tei)*
suspension of a driver's license

通信販売 → 通販
(tsū-shin-han-bai) *(tsū-han)*
mail-order sales

バス停留所 → バス停
(ba-su-tei-ryū-jo) *(ba-su-tei)*
bus stop

特別番組 → 特番
(toku-betsu-ban-gumi) *(toku-ban)*
special T.V. program

特別急行 → 特急
(toku-betsu-kyū-kō) *(tokkyū)*
special express train

最終電車 → 終電
(sai-shū-den-sha) *(shū-den)*
last train

パーソナル → パソコン
コンピューター *(pa-so-ko-n)*
(pā-so-na-ru-ko-n-pyū-tā)
personal computer

FOUR CHARACTER COMPOUNDS
よく使われる四文字熟語

There are many compounds composed of four kanji. Some of these are ancient Chinese proverbs and some are Japanese inventions created to teach morals or fit a particular situation. Many are derived from complicated stories.

異口同音
(i-ku-dō-on)
unanimously

同
— same

音
— sound

This compound translates directly as "different mouths, same sound". It refers to a group of people agreeing to something "unanimously".

一獲千金
(ikkaku-sen-kin)
to strike it rich

獲
— benefit

Translated directly this one means: "one benefit, one thousand gold bars".

一石二鳥
(isseki-ni-chō)
to kill two birds with one stone

石
— stone

鳥
— bird

The meaning and use of this expression is identical to its English equivalent: to do or gain two things from one action.

一挙両得
(ikkyo-ryō-toku)
same as above

挙
— hand

両
— both

得
— benefit

This translates directly as "one stroke, both benefits".

174

傍目八目
(oka-mé-hachi-moku)
everything is clearer when seen objectively.

傍
— side

目
— eye/also means a *go* stone

This expression is based on the game of *go* 碁. In *go*, players take turns placing white and black stones on a board in order to occupy territory. Translated directly this means "side view, eight moves". It refers to the fact that an objective observer of a *go* game can usually see the direction of play more clearly than those involved in the game.

温故知新
(on-ko-chi-shin)
the past holds the answers to the future

温故
— to study the past

知
— knowledge

新
— new

This proverb reminds us that the past offers us endless knowledge and the ability to gain a new perspective on our environment.

我田引水
(ga-den-in-sui)
self-centered

我
— self

田
— rice paddy

引
— to pull

This combination translates directly as "to carry water to my paddy". It refers to someone who is only interested in his own profit and attempts to better himself at the expense of others.

呉越同舟
(go-etsu-dō-shū)
bitter enemies in the same boat

呉・越
— ancient nations in China

同
— same

舟
— boat

The inspiration for this expression can be found in the ancient feud between two nations in ancient China that shared a border. This expression is used to describe the meeting of two opposing sides in one location.

五里霧中
(go-ri-mu-chū)
to be completely lost

里
— an archaic
unit of
measurement
equal to
3.9 km

霧
— fog

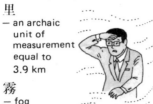

This combination describes someone who is lost in the middle of an area of thick fog that spreads in all directions. It is also used abstractly to mean ''to be at a loss''.

四捨五入
(shi-sha-go-nyū)
to round off numbers

捨
— to discard
入
— to put in

$$10,2$$
$$\downarrow$$
$$10$$

$$31,5$$
$$\downarrow$$
$$32$$

When rounding off numbers in Japan, as in the West, four and under are rounded down (discarded) and 5 and up are rounded up (put in).

針小棒大
(shin-shō-bō-dai)
to make a mountain out of a molehill

針
— needle
棒
— pole

Translated directly this reads ''small needle/large pole''. It is used for the process of describing something as small and unimportant as a needle in a way so as to make it seem like a pole.

弱肉強食
(jaku-niku-kyō-shoku)
survival of the fittest

弱
— weak
肉
— meat
強
— strong

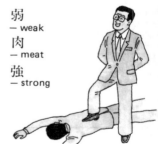

This compound's meaning is very clear: ''weak meat'' (weak animals) are the ''food'' of the ''strong''.

晴耕雨読
(sei-kō-u-doku)

to work in the fields on fine days
and read books on rainy days

晴
— clear weather

耕
-to till

読
— to read

This describes the ideal life for a
lover of books. One should live in
the country on his own farm, till
the soil when the weather permits
and read by the fire when it rains.

雲散霧消
(un-san-mu-shō)

to vanish like mist

雲
— cloud

散
— to scatter

霧
— fog

消
— to vanish

Just as clouds clear up and fog
seems to lift in only a few seconds,
human emotions and complica-
tions often fade in an instant.

以心伝心
(i-shin-den-shin)

nonverbal communication,
telepathy

以
— by means of

心
— heart

伝
— to
    transmit

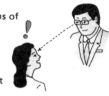

According to Buddhist precepts, a
master can teach his followers
better with deeds and emotions
than with words. This expression
describes such direct, nonverbal
transmissions.

疑心暗鬼
(gi-shin-an-ki)

a suspicious heart breeds paranoia

疑
— suspicion

鬼
— an imagined
    devil,
    unfounded
    anxiety

This describes the tendency for
people who are naturally suspicious or those who have had a bad
experience to fear shadows in the
dark and be wary of the unknown.

日常語の和英対照表

Numbers

1	*(ichi)*
2	*(ni)*
3	*(san)*
4	*(yon, shi)*
5	*(go)*
6	*(roku)*
7	*(nana, shichi)*
8	*(hachi)*
9	*(kyū, ku)*
10	*(jū, tō)*
11	*(jū-ichi)*
12	*(jū-ni)*
20	*(ni-jū)*
21	*(ni-jū-ichi)*
30	*(san-jū)*
40	*(yon-jū)*
100	*(hyaku)*
101	*(hyaku-ichi)*
175	*(hyaku-nana-jū-go)*
200	*(ni-hyaku)*
1000	*(sen)*
2000	*(ni-sen)*
10000	*(ichi-man)*
12345	*(ichi-man-ni-sen-san-byaku-yon-jū-go)*
20000	*(ni-man)*
100000	*(jū-man)*

Months

1 月	*(ichi-gatsu)*	January
2 月	*(ni-gatsu)*	February
3 月	*(san-gatsu)*	March
4 月	*(shi-gatsu)*	April
5 月	*(go-gatsu)*	May
6 月	*(roku-gatsu)*	June
7 月	*(shichi-gatsu)*	July
8 月	*(hachi-gatsu)*	August
9 月	*(ku-gatsu)*	September
10 月	*(jū-gatsu)*	October
11 月	*(jū-ichi-gatsu)*	November
12 月	*(jū-ni-gatsu)*	December

Months when used as a period of time

1 ヵ月 *(ikka-getsu)*
　　= *(hito-tsuki)* one month
2 ヵ月 *(ni-ka-getsu)*
　　= *(futa-tsuki)* two months
3 ヵ月 *(san-ka-getsu)*
　　= *(mi-tsuki)* three months
4 ヵ月 *(yon-ka-getsu)* four months

The Seasons

春	*(haru)*	Spring
夏	*(natsu)*	Summer
秋	*(aki)*	Autumn
冬	*(fuyu)*	Winter

The days of the month

1日	*(tsuitachi)*	the 1st
2日	*(futsuka)*	the 2nd
3日	*(mikka)*	the 3rd
4日	*(yokka)*	the 4th
5日	*(itsuka)*	the 5th
6日	*(muika)*	the 6th
7日	*(nanoka)*	the 7th
8日	*(yōka)*	the 8th
9日	*(kokonoka)*	the 9th
10日	*(tōka)*	the 10th
11日	*(jū-ichi-nichi)*	the 11th
12日	*(jū-ni-nichi)*	the 12th
13日	*(jū-san-nichi)*	the 13th
14日	*(jū-yokka)*	the 14th
15日	*(jū-go-nichi)*	the 15th
16日	*(jū-roku-nichi)*	the 16th
17日	*(jū-shichi-nichi)*	the 17th
18日	*(jū-hachi-nichi)*	the 18th
19日	*(jū-ku-nichi)*	the 19th
20日	*(hatsuka)*	the 20th
21日	*(ni-jū-ichi-nichi)*	the 21st
24日	*(ni-jū-yokka)*	the 24th
30日	*(san-jū-nichi)*	the 30th
31日	*(san-jū-ichi-nichi)*	the 31st

The days of the week

日曜日	*(nichi-yō-bi)*	Sunday
月曜日	*(getsu-yō-bi)*	Monday
火曜日	*(ka-yō-bi)*	Tuesday
水曜日	*(sui-yō-bi)*	Wednesday
木曜日	*(moku-yō-bi)*	Thursday
金曜日	*(kin-yō-bi)*	Friday
土曜日	*(do-yō-bi)*	Saturday

Time

1秒	*(ichi-byō)*	1 second
2秒	*(ni-byō)*	2 seconds
1分	*(ippun)*	1 minute
2分	*(ni-hun)*	2 minutes
1時間	*(ichi-ji-kan)*	1 hour
2時間	*(ni-ji-kan)*	2 hours
1分30秒	*(ippun-san-jū-byō)*	
		1 min. 30 sec.

昨日 *(saku-jitsu, kinō)*	yesterday
今日 *(kyō)*	today
明日 *(myō-nichi, ashita, asu)*	
	tomorrow

一昨日 *(issaku-jitsu, ototoi)* — the day before yesterday

明後日 *(myō-go-nichi, asatté)* — the day after tomorrow

今週、今月、今年
(kon-shū, kon-getsu, ko-toshi) this week, this month, this year

先週、先月、去年
(sen-shū, sen-getsu, kyo-nen) last week, last month, last year

来週、来月、来年
(rai-shū, rai-getsu, rai-nen) next week, next month, next year

Colors

赤 *(aka)*	red	黒 *(kuro)*	black
青 *(ao)*	blue	白 *(shiro)*	white
黄色 *(ki-iro)*	yellow	金色 *(kin-iro)*	gold
緑 *(midori)*	green	銀色 *(gin-iro)*	silver
茶色 *(cha-iro)*	brown	紫 *(murasaki)*	purple

Family

The equivalent expressions on the right side are polite forms to be used when referring to people not in one's family.

男	*(otoko)*	man		
女	*(onna)*	woman		
少年	*(shō-nen)*	young boy		
少女	*(shō-jo)*	young girl		
赤ちゃん	*(aka-chan)*	infant		
子供	*(kodomo)*	child	お子さん	*(o-ko-san)*
父	*(chichi)*	father	お父さん	*(o-tō-san)*
母	*(haha)*	mother	お母さん	*(o-kā-san)*
両親	*(ryō-shin)*	parents	ご両親	*(go-ryō-shin)*
夫	*(otto)*	husband	ご主人	*(go-shu-jin)*
妻	*(tsuma)*	wife	奥さん	*(oku-san)*
兄	*(ani)*	older brother	お兄さん	*(o-ni-i-san)*
弟	*(otōto)*	younger brother	弟さん	*(otōto-san)*
兄弟	*(kyō-dai)*	brothers and sisters	ご兄弟	*(go-kyō-dai)*
姉	*(ané)*	older sister	お姉さん	*(o-né-é-san)*
妹	*(imōto)*	younger sister	妹さん	*(imōto-san)*
姉妹	*(shimai)*	sisters	ご姉妹	*(go-kyō-dai)*
息子	*(musuko)*	son	息子さん	*(musuko-san)*
娘	*(musumé)*	daughter	娘さん	*(musumé-san)*
甥	*(oi)*	nephew	甥御さん	*(oi-go-san)*
姪	*(mei)*	niece	姪御さん	*(mei-go-san)*
叔父	*(oji)*	uncle	叔父さま	*(oji-sama)*
叔母	*(oba)*	aunt	叔母さま	*(oba-sama)*
祖父	*(so-fu)*	grandfather	お祖父さん	*(o-ji-i-san)*
祖母	*(so-bo)*	grandmother	お祖母さん	*(o-ba-a-san)*

* INDEX *

181

英文 **日本絵とき事典**

ILLUSTRATED
JAPANESE CHARACTERS

初 版 発 行　1989年7月25日
改訂15版　2009年2月1日
　　　　　　（Feb. 1, 2009, 15th edition）
編 集 人　黒澤明夫
発 行 人　江頭　誠
発 行 所　JTBパブリッシング
印 刷 所　JTB印刷

企画・編集　海外情報部
取材・編集協力　テクスタイド
イ ラ ス ト　松下正己
表紙デザイン　東　芳純
翻　　　訳　Lawrence B. Greenberg

●JTBパブリッシング
〒162-8446　東京都新宿区払方町25-5
編集：03-6888-7878
販売：03-6888-7893
広告：03-6888-7831
http://www.jtbpublishing.com/

●旅とおでかけ旬情報
http://rurubu.com/

084213　　712133
ISBN978-4-533-01359-1